Cafe Glacé
patty melt with chil
S0-BNF-765

The After Work Entertaining Cookbook

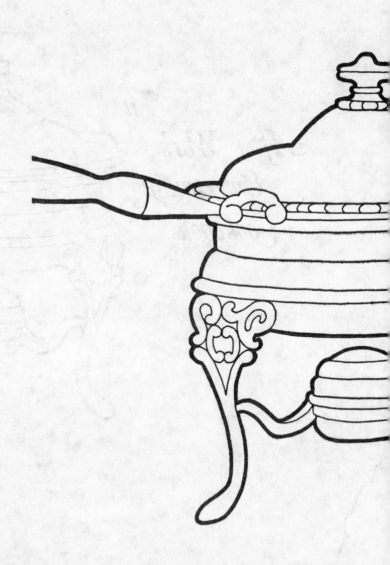

The After Work Entertaining Cookbook

CEIL DYER

DAVID McKAY COMPANY ■ NEW YORK

*Thanks to
the Oster Company
for their cooperation
and the use
of their blenders.*

Contents

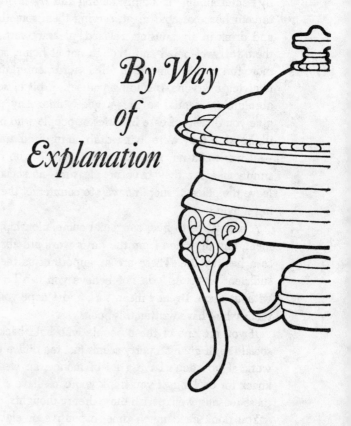

*By Way
of
Explanation*

◆

Before I began this book I tried to find a word to replace "entertaining," one that would say more accurately what I had in mind. Unfortunately, there just doesn't seem to be one. Let me tell you right here and now that I do not mean anything stuffy, formal, formidable, or even slightly serious by this word. What I do mean by "entertaining" is simply having fun by inviting your friends to your house or apartment; serving them something good to eat and drink in an amusing, relaxed, pleasant sort of way; making them feel welcomed and, though not at home, someplace that is more fun at the moment. In other words, entertaining in my book is giving everyone, including yourself, a bit of something that is absolutely essential to life—a good time. Any psychologist can give you dozens of case histories of people who became ill, really ill, because they were living drab, uninspired, uninteresting lives —all work and no play. There are people who fail at their jobs simply because they have no pleasure—no social life after they leave the office or shop, no way to counteract the tension of making a living.

A nice place to live, congenial companionship, relaxed amusement, and diversion from the day's work are absolutely essential to a healthy life. These are as important as the right food and sufficient exercise; I do not believe you can be truly successful without them. I really mean this, and I hope you agree, because that's why I have written this book.

If you are one of those people who hold back from an active social life; if giving a party seems just too difficult after a week of work; if you don't have a lot of money, an elegant house, or a knack for cooking; if you think you can't have a party for any of these reasons, well, perish those dreary thoughts!

You don't need much time, expensive or elaborate food, servants to help, or a luxurious setting; all you need is a flair for enjoyment. If you don't have it, it's something you can learn. It takes practice—but why not start tonight?

When I gave a party just after I had returned to a full-time job, there was a mad scramble for days before the event—shopping, cleaning, and cooking—both after work and on weekends. Even if everything went smoothly I was just too tired to enjoy the results. But often the meal was late and my guests had too many drinks while I worked frantically, preparing what I thought was expected of me in the way of a party meal.

Gradually, however, I caught on to the fact that I need not do "the expected," that the old-fashioned formulas I had been using were totally outdated and that there were new ones to replace them—new ways to cook, to serve, and to entertain successfully. Actually, these new ways were patterns that had evolved from today's life-style, patterns that resulted in great parties and suited to perfection the "after-hours" host or hostess who worked —for charity, for art, or, like me, simply for a paycheck.

This book has been written around these party patterns. Easy to give, fun to attend, they are America's favorite forms of entertaining.

THE HIGH COST OF DINING

In these days of spiraling prices, there are no inexpensive foods. Everything is priced high, higher, or outrageous and, to paraphrase a recent best-seller, the only defense is to dine well, to eat the best and only the best. If you think your paycheck won't support this theory, think again. The truth is that the best, more often than not, costs less than second rate. The trick is to know what really is best and to demand it, never accepting less.

Because what you *don't* know about good food *can* hurt you and your budget—great meats are not just a matter of cooking but also of buying—and because as a working person you don't have the time or the money (who does?) to waste on costly mistakes, I've tried throughout this book to give not just recipe directions but directions for buying the necessary ingredients as well as directions for planning the meal for the least work and the best results.

As I'm sure you know from your job, it's expertise, not physical work, that pays off in both hours and money saved, either in a job well done or in a meal that's perfection.

HOW TO CHART A SMOOTH PARTY COURSE

To chart a smooth party course begin with the familiar—what you know how to do you will do well—then add to your repertoire. Every party should have something new, an element of surprise and freshness. This need not be anything elaborate, expensive, exotic, or difficult to do; certainly it should not be too "far-out" for your particular guests but it should be a diversion from everyday.

For instance, if you have never given a party before, if yours is a junior executive income, and if you only know how to cook scrambled eggs, you might start with a "Sunday brunch-lunch."

Set your table where the early afternoon sun streams into the room, or on a sunny terrace, and fill the house with as many country flowers as your budget will allow. Your menu could begin with well-chilled whiskey sours (made from a mix), go on to your own specialty, scrambled eggs, served with the best bakery croissants your money can buy, and then end with a coffee spectacular. Not just powder stirred into hot water but flaming cafe diable, authentic Greek coffee, or espresso made in a real Italian espresso machine. Any one of these brews is easy to make, yet festive and fun—entertaining party fare for a finale that your reviewers will remember.

You really don't need a lot of special equipment. In fact, too many pots, pans, electric gadgets, etc. often only result in more things to clean, and who wants that? Here is a basic list of what I consider absolutely necessary, plus a list of "nice-to-haves." You can prepare any of the recipes in this book with the basic list, or make it easier with the extras.

NEEDED HERE AND NOW

Two big ceramic-coated cast-iron pots with close-fitting lids in the 4- and 6-quart sizes—the larger is sufficient for a recipe that serves 10 to 12. The best quality available; it pays off. Use for pasta, stew, braising meat, poaching ham, making stock, poaching chicken, etc.

A *2-quart double boiler*—the glass ones are preferable because you can see what's going on top and bottom. Use for custards and sauces, as separate saucepans for vegetables, rice, etc.

A *10-inch skillet*—preferably ceramic-coated cast iron. Here, too, top quality is the only kind worth buying. Use for frittata, bacon, sausages, corned-beef hash, country-fried potatoes, eggs, etc.

A *small 5- to 6-inch omelet or crêpe pan*—again, my preference is for ceramic-coated cast iron. Use for 2 or 3 egg omelets and crêpes, but I'm not such a purist that I won't use mine for sautéing onions, shallots, mushrooms, and the like.

An *open roasting pan*—one that measures 14 x 8.4 inches will accommodate a large chicken or a small turkey. Corning makes a wonderful one of opaque glass that's easy to clean and attractive enough to double as a serving dish. Use for roasting chicken, turkey, or meat, also as a lasagne pan for a big party.

Saucepans with glass lids—those that can be used on top of the stove or in the oven, that can go from refrigerator or freezer straight to the stove, that can be used as serving dishes as well. I like those made of Pyroceram, also made by Corning. They are available in sizes ranging from 2 to 6 quarts.

Soufflé mold—the 2-quart size is the most practical for soufflés, of course, but also useful for any baked casserole.

Three or more layer-cake pans—for layer cakes when I feel in such an expansive mood, but also handy for such diverse uses as heating rolls and crisping bacon in the oven, as well as for many other baking uses.

Baking sheets—yes, I do bake cookies, but these are handy, too, for hors d'oeuvres, cracker crisping, etc.

A *dependable easy-to-clean stove*—one with 2 ovens, if possible.

An *adequate refrigerator*—one with a large frozen-food compartment.

Real butcher knives—I have 3, all essential—a serrated-edge, razor-sharp carver; a broad-bladed chopping knife; and a medium-sized utility knife for paring and slicing.

Long-handled wooden spoons—2, at least, for stirring and blending.

French wire whisk—an absolute essential to me because there is no comparable way to whip eggs or to smooth out a sauce.

Spatula—for all the obvious reasons.

Long-handled fork—same as above.

Cheese grater—just a plain old-fashioned 4-sided grater works fine.

Can opener and bottle opener—the common variety, much cheaper and easier to clean than the electric marvels.

Wooden chopping board.

Set of mixing bowls—at least 3, preferably 4.

You will note that almost everything suggested above serves double duty. To my way of thinking there simply isn't time, money, or space for single-purpose equipment.

NICE TO HAVE

Electric blender—this heads my list; wonderful for drinks, homemade mayonnaise, feather-light crêpes, a whole range of gelatin desserts, mousses, and creams, puréed vegetables, etc.

Electric mixer—not essential unless you often bake homemade cakes or mash lots of potatoes, but it does cut down on work if you really get serious about cooking. The portable hand mixer is easier to clean, takes less space, and is just as useful as the super deluxe models.

A garbage disposal—this, as you will probably notice, is my favorite appliance; I had one installed in my rented apartment. If your local ordinances don't prohibit it, I strongly recommend saving on lunches and taxis to pay for one. Gone forever is the messy, smelly job of getting rid of garbage.

Dishwasher—for the serious party giver, a great time and work saver, and it does make cleaning up twice as fast.

Self-cleaning oven—really marvelous if your idea of cookery is roast meat or broiled steak.

Portable electric broiler—great for toast, hors d'oeuvres, broiled hamburgers, frankfurters, shish kebabs, and such.

Electric skillet or chafing dish—for cook-at-the-table meals.

A *super refrigerator*—self-defrosting, with lots of room for frozen and fresh food, and equipped for making and storing loads of ice.

Electric hot trays—great for keeping everything just ready to eat without any frantic maneuvers on your part.

SETTING THE TABLE

Now as for china, glass, silver, table linen, etc., it's everyone for himself as to design, price, color, and so forth. I have found a few rules of thumb that work for me and I pass them on with the thought that no one is going to force you to follow them.

Generally speaking, "less is more" when it comes to china, glass, and linen. Unadorned good-quality crystal still looks good long after the flowered, etched, decorated "what-have-you's" have bored you to tears. You don't need a great deal—8 wineglasses and 8 "on-the-rocks" will see you through most small to medium-sized parties. For bigger bashes it's insane to use crystal. Substitute those silver-coated plastic ones or glass mugs from the dime store or paper—there is a lot of attractive solid-color paper stuff around that is perfectly acceptable. The same is true for china or earthenware. If you have the money for bone china, you'll be a lot happier with a simple pattern that you can vary with different table decorations. A few years ago, someone gave me 8 beautiful English bone china plates and 8 matching dessert or salad plates. The pattern is delicate and charming, and for months I couldn't use it often enough; then suddenly I felt if I had to look at those itsy-bitsy flowers one more time, I'd scream. I simply couldn't wait to take my next paycheck to Bloomingdale's department store and buy a whole service of spartan plain Dansk-ware. It's absolutely unadorned and is a lovely creamy khaki color that looks heavenly with all sorts of different-colored napkins and table settings. Imagine, for example, a summer table set with pale beige plates and sky-blue linen napkins, centered by an antique basket filled with daisies and cornflowers.

As for silver, if your grandmother left a whole service to you or you are lucky enough to afford real silver, there's nothing nicer. Here's where to let yourself go if you like a richly patterned effect. Real silver can take elaborate pattern and not get boring. I have some heavily decorated knives and forks that look great even with the Dansk-ware. I hasten to add they were a handsome gift.

If you can't or don't want to spend for sterling, there is nothing to be upset about. Today some of the choicest tables set by some of the richest hostesses use stainless steel by preference, not by necessity. Stainless steel is a wonderful modern material for cutlery. It is not, however, an imitation of silver, and only when it tries to be is it in bad taste. Look for clean modern design in stainless, or play up its twentieth-century look by selecting clear Lucite or ceramic bamboo handles. Again, service for 8 plus 8 extra forks and dessert spoons for a big buffet is plenty. More than 16 people? I use throw-away plastic.

Serving utensils can be anything that suits you and your house. Serve soup with a big speckled enamelware ladle, use wooden spoons for casserole dishes, antique odd spoons for anything spoonable. The idea is to get out of a rut and open your mind to the look of today, not stick to the tired traditions of a bygone generation.

Finally, a note on linen. I rarely use tablecloths, except when I set up several small tables for a big party; then I whip up to-the-floor versions in inexpensive cottons or felt. I concentrate instead on a variety of good-looking napkins in an assortment of colors and fabrics, anything from heavy cream-colored linen for a more formal table to checked gingham and calico prints. Used with imaginative baskets of flowers, seasonal fruits, or even vegetables, they give a fabulous effect on a bare polished table. Needless to say, it's a lot easier to wash and iron a dozen napkins than a banquet-sized damask tablecloth. No, thank you, I have better things to do. More than 12 napkins? Well, I'll go as high as 16, but beyond that it's good-looking paper and nobody seems to care.

THE MORNING AFTER AND WHAT TO DO ABOUT IT

Between you and me, I really don't think the reason most working people hesitate to give parties is time or money. The time for the fun part, and for shopping, cooking, and preparing, can usually be found, and, as you'll read in this book, even big parties can have little price tags. No, these are not the reasons. The real reason for "party holdouts" is that everyone, and I mean everyone, hates to face the horrendous mess in the kitchen when the last merrymaker has departed. Leave it until the next morning and it really is a disaster area. So most people face the weary job of washing dishes, scrubbing pots, emptying the garbage, etc., etc., way into the small hours. Result? One feels like "having been drug through a knothole" all the next day, and the firm resolve "never to do it again" takes hold once more.

It need not be—no, really, even if you lack some of the more elaborate cleaning equipment such as a dishwasher and a garbage disposal, nice as they are to have. The real secret is simply this: *clean as you go.* Sounds easier than it is? No, it is really only a matter of habit. If you train yourself to wash, dry, and put away automatically as you cook and prepare a meal, the difference can be astounding. It is, after all, simple enough to rinse out 1 bowl and wash 1 fork after you have mixed the salad dressing. But if you leave these plus the equipment you used to make the salad plus the salad bowl, plates, and forks used to serve, and add to this the chopping board and ingredient containers—salt, pepper, oil bottle, spices, etc.—to put away, you have the makings of a major mess.

Another rule is: *use the same utensil over again.* This is one of my favorite work-saving rules. For example, let's say you are having rice and peas. Cook the rice and place it in a colander over simmering water until you are ready to serve it (it'll taste better for waiting). Now rinse out the pot the rice was cooked in, don't wash it, and use it to cook the peas. When done—don't overcook —you want them just barely tender—drain and add to the rice. Now wash, dry, and put away the pot you've used for both peas and rice. At cleanup time all you really have left to do is to wash the colander. The water pot under the colander need only be drained, dried, and put away. See what I mean?

The next rule is: *let it clean itself.* This applies to such horrendous jobs as broilers, sticky roast pans, pots that have been used for clinging custards, pie tins, pans used for sugary desserts like baked apples, etc. As soon as the cooked dish is ready, transfer it to a serving platter and keep warm in a low oven or on a hot tray. If it's a roast it will taste better and be easier to carve if allowed to cool a bit. Or cool the dish if it is to be served cold. Now quickly take that dirty, crusty pot, pan, or whatever, put it in the sink, fill with hot water, and add a generous handful of dishwasher powder. Yes, dishwasher powder, even if you don't have a dishwasher. Let it soak for an hour or so while you go about your own affairs, or even until the party is over. Rinse out with hot water and there you are—like magic the sticky, greasy, burned-on food is gone, the pan is sparkling clean, and it takes only seconds to rinse, dry, and put away.

All of the above is what I call "preventive cleaning"—like preventive medicine, it's lots more pleasant than waiting for the critical stage to set in. However, no matter how well you manage to keep Rules One, Two, and Three, you can't grab plates out of your guests' hands and wash them while they stand there emptyhanded. So, inevitably, when the party's over there is the job of washing plates, serving dishes, glasses, ashtrays, etc., but it need not be a big job if you follow a system. First, get rid of the garbage. To me a garbage disposal is the most treasured appliance, more important than a dishwasher. If you have one, scrape everything into the sink and turn it on. No disposal? Then everything goes into one of those heavy-duty plastic bags, to be closed tightly and stashed away. Now if you have a double sink fill one side with very hot water and plenty of detergent, or, if yours is a small "apartment-sized" kitchen with a single sink, use a large dish pan. Add a few drops of ammonia (it cuts the grease). Rinse plates, glasses, etc. with cold water and stack neatly in the hot soapy wash. Let them soak a bit while you wash the silver separately and place it in a dish rack to drain. Now, wearing rubber gloves, drain the soapy water off the glasses and dishes and rinse with the hottest possible water. Let them dry themselves while you "neat up" the living and dining rooms and sweep the kitchen. Wipe off the stove and countertops, put away the now dry dishes, and that's it. Needless to say, if you have a dishwasher everything is that much easier, but I have coped with huge parties equipped only with my three rules, dishwasher powder, a dish rack, and lots of hot water. The answer is the same principle you use in your job: organization, logic, and some basic equipment. It's brain, not brawn, that gets the job done.

HAVING PEOPLE OVER FOR A DRINK

We still call it a cocktail party, but the word as well as the original party idea is out of date. Cocktails are sometimes served, but the drinks are more often something else—plain Scotch and soda or vodka and orange juice, tall, cool drinks made with wine or icy cold steins of beer. These days no one wants to stand in a crowded room sipping something watery from a stemmed glass, munching limp little bite-sized sandwiches. The truth is, I don't believe anyone ever did.

"Come-by-for-a-drink" hospitality is no longer limited to the traditional hours of 5 to 7 o'clock in the evening, which doesn't mean that people are drinking more, only differently. Beer and wine parties that include fairly substantial fare are Friday or Saturday all-evening get-togethers. "Come for drinks" can be as simple as just whiskey and soda and "stay for a casserole supper," or it can mean a smorgasbord meal, with a variety of hot and cold dishes and your choice of drinks, plus coffee and a special dessert.

To my way of thinking, it's ridiculous to put any pressure on yourself after work unless it's absolutely necessary; there's enough of that during the day. Having people over for a drink shouldn't disintegrate into an expensive show-off kind of party but should be simply a pleasurable gathering of friends. It should be fun for the people who come and a bit more "special" than everyday, but you shouldn't be whacked out financially by what you serve or worn down to a frazzle by preparing it.

Here are some things you can do to make having people over for a drink both easy and fun. Set up your bar, then let everyone make his own drinks. Let guests get into the act by shelling their own cocktail peanuts, popping their own corn, or barbecuing their own meat.

Use paper plates and napkins; they come in great colors these days. For a large crowd buy and use those new "silver-look" plastic glasses; they are inexpensive, reusable, and nonbreakable.

Have your party in the most pleasurable and comfortable part of the house—a big cheerful kitchen or a game room, on a terrace, in the backyard, or at your place of work if it suits your style.

Keep within your food and drink budget or you won't enjoy the party, but think of ways to serve that add a party touch. If you can't afford to serve more than 1 or 2 drinks, make them very special ones and make a production of the making—shake with crushed ice in a 1920s silver or silver-plated shaker, or put your blender to use.

Have people to your house before or after another party. It heightens the entire evening for everyone, but as people can't stay long or have more than 1 drink (or 1 and a refill), the cost is negligible.

You don't need a lot of money or time for good parties. You don't need a completely stocked bar or an assortment of elaborate hot and cold food. You don't need expensive or elaborate bar equipment. All you do need is a little talent, natural or acquired, for having and giving a good time.

You can, of course, "call in sick" at work, then spend the entire day "getting everything ready," or, with a little pre-thought and planning, you can put the whole works together—great food and drink, party mood, and ambiance—within 30 minutes or less. The trick is to know yourself, what you can do, and keep within that range. Suit the party to your life and the style of your house or apartment. In other words, do only what you can achieve easily with the equipment and props you have on hand.

Here's a spate of parties that prove my points. They were not given by me so I can brag, but by some very great friends, all people who know how to put in a hard day's work, then forget it for an evening of fun.

You certainly won't want to use their party ideas in total, but I do think you will find here, as I did, a goodly amount of entertaining ways to adapt to your own needs.

A Beer
and Peanuts
Party

◆

A congenial kitchen-dining-family room, big and spacious, with an early-American hutch painted deep blue, country French chairs and table, deep red tile floor.

THE MENU

Roasted Peanuts, Hot from the Oven
Thick Slices of Sharp Cheddar Cheese

Assorted Imported Beers

Crisp Cool Apple Slices
Cherry Tomatoes
Seasoned Salt for Dunking

THE SPECIAL PROPS

A weather-beaten, old-fashioned washtub found at a flea market. Heavy-stemmed, thick glasses from a wholesale restaurant-supply store. An antique straw basket from the same flea market, with a red and white bandana to line it.

PARTY STRATEGY

Buy an assortment of imported beers in deep green and amber brown bottles—no cans, please. Refrigerate until just before serving.

On the way home from work pick up 1 or 2 large bags of crushed ice. Dump the ice in the washtub and place the cold beer in it as well as the glasses.

Start the peanuts roasting; they may not be ready when your

guests arrive, but they will smell marvelous. They can be served hot from the oven after everyone has had his first glass of beer. Slice the cheese and apples and arrange on a serving plate. Wash cherry tomatoes, then put in a bowl and fill another smaller bowl with seasoned salt. The peanuts make an entrance in the bandana-lined basket; everyone shells his own.

◆

ROASTED PEANUTS

Put 2 or 3 quarts dried peanuts still in hulls on 1 or 2 baking sheets. Place in a preheated 375° F. oven to roast for 25 to 35 minutes, or until really crunchy. Stir and turn once or twice while roasting. Serve hot in the shell.

A Beer
Garden
Get-Together

◆

THE SETTING

A freewheeling game room with a long, polished wood bar, brown leather chairs, and an old, round country table large enough to seat a crowd comfortably in front of a big roaring fire in an open brick fireplace.

THE MENU

Hot Buttered Freshly Popped Popcorn
Thin-Sliced Paprika Salami

Draft Beer

Party Rye Bread
German-Style Sliced Tomatoes
Crocks of Hot Mustard
Sweet-and-Sour Beans with Frankfurters

THE SPECIAL PROPS

The beer itself in a keg (available at your liquor store); the popcorn kernels in long-handled popping pans for guests to hold over the fire and pop their own bowlfuls. Old-world beer steins, the best you can find and afford, or glass ones from the five-and-ten-cent store. A big wooden bread board for the salami and bread. A good-looking oven-to-table ceramic-coated cast-iron pot for the beans and a wooden spoon to serve them. Small earthenware plates, oversized paper napkins, and country kitchen forks to eat the beans.

PARTY STRATEGY

Buy the salami and black bread from a good delicatessen and have it machine-sliced paper thin.

—

Order the keg or kegs of beer several days in advance.

While someone else sees to the fire in the fireplace, put the popcorn kernels in the pans with fresh butter (not the packet of oil that is sometimes found in the package) and set up the bar and buffet table.

About 30 minutes before guests are due to arrive, prepare the bean casserole and put it in the oven. Then prepare the tomatoes.

◆

SWEET-AND-SOUR BEANS WITH FRANKFURTERS

2 slices of bacon
1 large onion, peeled and chopped
2 cans (1 pound each) baked beans
1 can (15½ ounces) kidney beans
1 can (15½ ounces) large lima beans
1 pound frankfurters, thinly sliced
1 cup catsup
¼ cup cider vinegar
¼ cup brown sugar
1 tablespoon prepared mustard

Fry the bacon until crisp in a large 2½- to 3-quart ceramic-coated cast-iron pot (one that can go to the table). Remove bacon, drain, crumble and set aside and pour off all but about 1 tablespoon fat. Add onion and cook, stirring, for 2 or 3 minutes. Remove pot from heat. Add beans, crumbled bacon and frankfurters. Combine remaining ingredients and gently stir into bean mixture. Cover and bake in preheated 375° F. oven for 30 minutes. Serve from the pot.

MAKES 10 TO 12 BUFFET SERVINGS.

◆

GERMAN-STYLE SLICED TOMATOES

5 or 6 large ripe but firm tomatoes
¼ cup sugar
1 teaspoon salt
3 tablespoons cider vinegar
4 tablespoons salad oil

Slice tomatoes as thin as possible. Arrange the slices slightly overlapping on a large platter. Sprinkle evenly with sugar, salt, vinegar, and oil. Let stand at room temperature for 15 minutes. Turn with a spatula. Refrigerate until ready to serve.

MAKES 8 SERVINGS.

A Sangría
Party on
a Terrace

♦

The terrace of a hilltop apartment in San Francisco; fanback wicker chairs and small wicker tables, lots of country baskets, shadowy fantail palms in redwood tubs, a fantastic view of the city.

THE MENU

Red and White Sangría

Assorted Tapas
(*Spanish hors d'oeuvres*)
Anticuchos
(*Latin-American barbecued beef cubes*)

THE SPECIAL PROPS

Four table-top hibachis, or 1 for each 2 guests, each glowing with live coals, each on its own small flagstone table. Two great Victorian pressed-glass pitchers. Double-sized highball glasses. A set of library steps, lacquered a deep cool green, instead of a buffet table for an assortment of tapas on green-leaf pottery plates.

PARTY STRATEGY

One day ahead prepare marinade for the *anticuchos*. Add meat and refrigerate. Prepare vegetables in vinaigrette dressing. Refrigerate. Prepare sangría base and refrigerate.

About 30 minutes before guests are due to arrive, drain vegetables and meat and arrange for serving. Mix sangrías and refrigerate. Add ice just before serving.

◆

TAPAS

Fresh figs, peeled and wrapped in paper-thin slices of dried beef. Imported canned white asparagus marinated in vinaigrette dressing, drained just before serving. Jumbo prunes plumped in boiling water, pitted, marinated in Spanish brandy, and drained just before serving. Spanish sardines in oil, drained, placed on toast strips that have been spread with mustard. Jumbo Spanish ripe olives. Artichoke hearts, canned, cut into halves, and filled with cream cheese mixed with red caviar.

◆

SANGRÍA BASE

2 large oranges, washed, chopped and seeded but not peeled
1 lime, washed, chopped and seeded but not peeled
1 lemon, washed, chopped and seeded but not peeled
2½ cups sugar
6 cups water
1 cup Spanish brandy or any good-quality dry brandy

Combine fruits, sugar, and water in a large saucepan. Stir over moderate heat until sugar dissolves. Let simmer over low heat for about 1½ hours, or until reduced to a bitter-sweet syrup. Cool. Add brandy and refrigerate until ready to use.

MAKES 2 CUPS.

◆

RED SANGRÍA

½ *cup sangría base*
2 *bottles* (*¾-quart size*) *Spanish Rioja or any good*
   dry red wine
1 *bottle* (*10 ounces*) *club soda*
Ice cubes
Paper-thin slices of lemon or lime
Fresh peach slices or quartered strawberries, or both

Have all ingredients well chilled. Combine base, wine, and club soda. Pour over ice in serving glasses. Add a slice of lemon or lime and a few pieces of fruit.

(Classically, the ice and fruit are added to the pitcher before serving. It's very pretty, but unless everyone is served at once, the punch becomes diluted by the melting ice.)

MAKES 2 QUARTS.

◆

WHITE SANGRÍA

Follow recipe for red sangría above but substitute a dry white wine.

◆

ANTICUCHOS

LATIN-AMERICAN BARBECUED BEEF CUBES
(An American Version)

2 *pounds top or bottom round of beef*

MARINADE
1 *cup red-wine vinegar*
1 *cup dry red wine*
3 *or 4 garlic cloves, peeled and cut into halves*
8 *or 10 fresh red chilies, cut into halves, with seeds removed*
1 *tablespoon ground cumin seeds*

SAUCE
1 *bottle (16 ounces) barbecue sauce*
Juice of 1 lemon
1 *cup marinade from beef*

Cut meat into small, bite-sized cubes. Place in a long, shallow nonmetal pan. Combine marinade ingredients and pour over meat. Cover and refrigerate from 12 to 24 hours, turning meat occasionally.

At least 1 hour before barbecuing, fill the hibachis with coals, ignite, and let burn until white ash appears on the surface of the fuel.

String meat cubes on small skewers, 3 or 4 pieces of meat on each. Combine sauce ingredients.

For each serving arrange 2 or 3 skewers and a small bowl of sauce on a small tray or plate. Let each guest broil his own *anticuchos* about 3 inches over glowing coals for 3 or 4 minutes, turning and basting them with sauce several times as they cook.
MAKES 6 SERVINGS.

*A Cocktail
Hour Before
Going on
to Dinner*

♦

One of Charleston's most fashionable decorating shops—a pot-pourri of Americana, English, and country French antiques. A showplace of fabric and furniture but with lots of comfort and a bit of humor.

THE MENU

Jimmy's Original Cyanide Special
or
Scotch and Soda

Jumbo Black Olives   *Radishes*
Florentine Spread
Water Biscuits
Hot Cheese and Ham Puffs

THE SPECIAL PROPS

On an English hunt table, a generous-sized black lacquer (plastic lookalike) tray with all the necessary equipment and in-gredients for preparing and serving this host's Cyanide Specials: electric blender, Toby jug for the orange juice, and pewter bowls —a large one for the ice cubes, smaller ones for lime wedges and cubes of sugar. Plus, of course, Scotch, soda, and glasses.

PARTY STRATEGY

Prepare Florentine Spread a day ahead to allow flavors to blend and to chill the mixture thoroughly.

About 20 minutes before guests are due to arrive, set up bar; then prepare and bake cheese and ham puffs.

NOTE: The Cyanide Specials are not as lethal as they sound,

just fun to make or watch being made. Icy cold, they taste great after a hard day's work—or anytime, for that matter.

◆

"PREPARED-TO-ORDER" CYANIDE SPECIALS

1 tablespoon frozen concentrated orange juice
Juice from a small wedge of lime, about ½ teaspoon
1 cube "tiny dot" sugar (or ½ cube of regular size)
1 ounce Scotch, or a little more
¼ cup club soda
3 or 4 ice cubes

Place ingredients in container of electric blender in order listed. Blend at high speed until ice is melted. Pour into serving glass while still frothy and icy cold. Serve at once.

MAKES 1 DRINK.

◆

FLORENTINE SPREAD OR DIP

1 package (10 ounces) frozen chopped spinach
Salt
Water
⅓ to ½ cup real mayonnaise
1 tablespoon fresh lemon juice
1 tablespoon grated onion
Dash of Tabasco

Cook spinach in salted water according to package directions. Drain in a colander, then press out all remaining water with the back of a wooden spoon. Place in a mixing bowl and add remaining ingredients, using sufficient mayonnaise to make a thick spread or dip. Refrigerate until well chilled.

MAKES 1½ CUPS.

◆

CHEESE AND HAM PUFFS

1 can (10 biscuits) refrigerator biscuits
3 ounces Smithfield ham spread or deviled ham
20 small cubes of mild Cheddar cheese

Preheat oven to 375° F.

Split each biscuit into halves. Make an indentation in each half and in it place a demitasse spoonful of ham spread and 1 cube of cheese. Bring dough up and around to enclose filling completely. Bake in preheated oven until lightly browned. Serve hot.

MAKES 20 PUFFS.

Soup
Suppers

◆

Tureen of Special Soup
Hot Breads
Cheese Tray   Fresh Fruit

Cognac

Coffee
Fine Chocolates

SOUP FOR A GOURMET SUPPER PARTY

As the world becomes more complex, our work more complicated, we Americans are learning to simplify our personal lives.
In so doing, we often enrich it by substituting quality for quantity. The current trend to casual come-as-you-are entertaining is
a perfect example.

Your menu can be a really great soup followed by cheese and
fruit, then coffee and a very light sweet. Don't think of a soup
supper as just being simple and economical, though it is, but as
a true gourmet feast, which it can be. This is the menu to serve
after a big game, after a day on the ski slopes, or, for that matter,
on any frosty day after work.

Bring the soup from the kitchen slightly steaming, its aroma
filling the room, in an old-fashioned ironstone tureen or a brightly
enameled soup pot. The only accompaniment necessary is good
honest bread—not the pale, soft packaged imitation, but such
breads as hearty sourdough from San Francisco, real French or
Italian loaves with crispy, crumbling crust, or honest corn bread
made from stone-ground meal.

The recipes that follow are for classic soups that everyone truly
enjoys, but made easy and, of course, always made ahead. Almost
all can be frozen so there's no work on the day of the party meal.
Follow the soup course with some really good cheese and fresh

fruit, and then end the meal with the best and freshest real coffee (not instant) your particular coffee maker can make.

◆

BLACK BEAN SOUP

1 *pound dried black beans*
Water
1 *tablespoon salt, for beans*
2 *garlic cloves*
1 *teaspoon salt, for soup*
1 *tablespoon Italian mixed herbs*
2 *tablespoons butter*
2 *onions, chopped*
½ *cup dry sherry*
6 *or 8 thin slices of avocado*
Thick slices of crusty French bread

Soak beans overnight in sufficient water to cover completely. Next day, add additional water to cover again by 1 inch. Add 1 tablespoon salt, bring to a boil, cover, and cook until beans are almost tender. (These beans require longer cooking than other varieties.)

Crush together garlic, 1 teaspoon salt, and the herbs. Heat butter in a large skillet. Add onions and sauté for about 5 minutes. Stir in seasoning mixture, then about ½ cup of the hot bean liquid. Cover and simmer for about 10 minutes. Add to beans and continue cooking until flavors are thoroughly blended, about 1 hour.

Remove 3 cups of beans and liquid to the container of your electric blender and blend until smooth. Return this to soup kettle. Add sherry. Check seasonings and correct if necessary.

Ladle into soup bowls or a serving tureen. Garnish top with thin slices of avocado. Serve with crusty French bread.

MAKES 6 TO 8 MAIN-COURSE SERVINGS.

◆

NEW ORLEANS BOUILLABAISSE

2½ pounds firm-fleshed fish fillets
Salt
Pepper
½ cup chopped onion
2 tablespoons finely minced garlic
½ cup chopped celery
¼ cup chopped parsley
1 can (1 pound) tomatoes
1 cup water
2 tablespoons freshly squeezed lemon juice
3 tablespoons Worcestershire sauce
¼ teaspoon spice Parisienne or allspice
3 or 4 dashes of Tabasco
2 tablespoons all-purpose flour
3 tablespoons butter
1 tablespoon oil
1½ pounds raw shrimps, shelled and deveined
1 pound crabmeat

Season fish fillets with salt and pepper. Combine the onion, garlic, celery, and parsley. Mix together the tomatoes, water, lemon juice, Worcestershire sauce, spice Parisienne (or allspice), and Tabasco. Knead flour with butter to form a paste.

Brush oil on bottom and sides of pot. A black iron pot with heavy lid is ideal for this, but any heavy pot or an electric skillet can be used. Place a layer of seasoned fish in the pot. Crumble some of the flour-butter mixture over the fish. Add a layer of vegetables next, then spoon some of the tomato mixture over. Repeat until all the fish, vegetable mixture, and tomato mixture are used. Size of the pot will determine the layers. Place the lid on the pot and cook over medium heat until juice starts to boil, then reduce immediately to low heat. Cook, covered, for 30 to 40 minutes, or until fish flakes easily with fork. About 10 minutes before stew is done, add shrimps and crabmeat.

MAKES 8 TO 10 MAIN-COURSE SERVINGS.

◆

OYSTER STEW

¼ pound butter
4 dozen oysters, with liquid
2 tablespoons Worcestershire sauce
Dash of Tabasco
1 teaspoon salt
Freshly ground black pepper
8 cups milk, or half milk and half cream
¼ cup cognac or other good brandy
½ cup minced parsley
Paprika
Butter
French bread slices

Heat the butter in a deep, heavy kettle. When it bubbles, add oysters, Worcestershire, Tabasco, and salt and pepper to taste. Cook gently until the edges of the oysters begin to curl, about 1 minute. Heat the milk until hot but not boiling; combine with the oysters and simmer briefly but do not boil. Add cognac. Let stand to blend the flavors. When ready to serve, heat until hot but not boiling. Pour into a warm tureen and top with minced parsley, paprika to taste, and dots of butter. Ladle over thick slices of French bread.

MAKES 8 MAIN-COURSE SERVINGS.

◆

BOULA BOULA

1 can (10¾ ounces) condensed cream of potato soup
1 can (10¾ ounces) condensed green pea soup
2½ cups milk
2 tablespoons Madeira wine
1 can (10 ounces) condensed green turtle soup
½ cup dry sherry
½ cup heavy cream
Salt
Pepper

Adjust broiler racks so that individual heatproof casseroles will be about 4 inches below the source of heat. Preheat broiler.

Combine potato and pea soups in a heavy saucepan. Add milk, place over low heat, and stir until mixture is smooth. Add Madeira and continue to cook, stirring often, until soup is very hot. Do not allow to boil.

Put the turtle soup in a second saucepan over moderate heat. Add the sherry and bring almost but not quite to boiling point.

Whip the heavy cream until it just begins to thicken. Season lightly with salt and pepper.

Pour potato-pea soup into deep individual heatproof casseroles. Pour turtle soup over surface of first soup without mixing. Spread the lightly whipped cream over top of turtle soup. Place casseroles immediately under direct broiler heat until surface is lightly browned. Serve at once.

MAKES 6 MAIN-COURSE SERVINGS.

◆

POTAGE MAISON

4 large white leeks, trimmed
2 large white turnips, peeled and cut into pieces
1 large carrot, scraped and sliced
2 large California "white" potatoes, peeled and chopped
2 cups clear chicken stock or broth
2 cups water
2 tablespoons butter
½ cup minced onion
1 tablespoon curry powder
Salt
Pepper
Sliced French bread

Combine leeks, turnips, carrot, potatoes, stock or broth, and water in a large soup pot. Bring to a full boil, then reduce heat and let simmer until vegetables are very tender, about 1 hour.

Remove vegetables with a slotted spoon and place in the container of an electric blender. Add a little of the cooking stock and blend for 1 second, or until the mixture reaches the consistency of a coarse purée. Return mixture to soup pot.

In a small saucepan melt the butter. Add the onion and let cook, stirring often, until onion is very limp, about 15 minutes. Stir in curry powder and cook again, stirring until blended. With a rubber spatula scrape onion and curry butter into soup pot. Season soup with salt and pepper to taste. Increase heat until soup is very hot. Serve over thick slices of toasted French bread.

MAKES 6 MAIN-COURSE SERVINGS.

◆

MINESTRONE

4 tablespoons butter
1 large purple onion, peeled and chopped
2 garlic cloves, peeled and minced
2 small chili peppers, minced
2 tablespoons minced parsley
1 cup chopped ham
8 cups chicken stock or broth
1 can (1 pound) Italian-style tomatoes with basil
Salt
1 large boiling potato, peeled and cut into bite-sized cubes
½ cup uncooked elbow macaroni
1 cup well-washed fresh spinach, packed down
½ cup freshly grated Parmesan cheese
Oregano
Freshly ground black pepper

Melt the butter in a large soup pot. Add onion, garlic, chili peppers, parsley, and ham. Sauté until all the onion is limp. Add
chicken stock or broth and tomatoes. Season lightly with salt. Let
simmer for about 30 minutes. Add potato and macaroni. Continue to cook until potato cubes are soft and macaroni tender.
Add spinach and bring to a full boil. Remove from heat and stir
in Parmesan cheese. Add additional salt, oregano, and pepper
to taste.

Pass additional grated Parmesan cheese at the table.

MAKES 6 TO 8 SERVINGS.

◆

LOUISIANA SEAFOOD GUMBO

4 tablespoons butter
¼ pound lean ham, diced
1 large purple onion, peeled and chopped
1 garlic clove, peeled and minced
1 small green pepper, seeded and chopped
2 or 3 celery ribs, chopped
1 tablespoon flour
1 can (1 pound) Italian-style tomatoes with basil
6 cups chicken stock or broth
Salt
Pepper
1 pint oysters and liquid
1 or 2 shrimp shells
1 pound raw shrimps, peeled and deveined
1 pound fresh or frozen lump crabmeat
1 tablespoon filé powder
4 cups cooked rice, approximately (see cooking
*   instructions page 181)*

Melt the butter in a soup pot. Add the ham, onion, garlic, green pepper, and celery. Sauté until vegetables are limp, about 10 minutes. Sprinkle with flour and stir for 1 or 2 minutes. Add tomatoes and stock. Season lightly with salt and pepper. Add liquid from oysters and the shrimp shells. Let simmer for 30 minutes. Add oysters, shrimps, and crabmeat. Bring to a full boil.

Can be made ahead to this point.

Remove from heat and stir in filé powder. Add additional salt and pepper if needed. Remove and discard shrimp shells. Ladle into large soup bowls over mounds of cooked rice.

MAKES 8 TO 12 SERVINGS.

*Big Parties
with Little
Price Tags
and Almost
No Work*

◆

KITCHEN HAMBURGER PARTY

THE MENU

Hamburger Patties Hot from the Grill
Hot Buttered Rolls

Cold Beer and Cokes

Shredded Lettuce   Crumbled Roquefort Cheese
Marinated Tomato and Onion Slices
Hot Cheese Rabbit   Chili Sauce
Chutney

Basket of Apples and Walnuts
Crisp Cookies
Frozen Peach Mousse
Coffee

I have found this "kitchen hamburger party" to be a great favorite. Who doesn't like a really good hamburger—one that you assemble yourself hot from the griddle with all the "fixings"! It's easy and it's fun and, what's more, even the cleaning up after is simple. Paper plates, cups, and napkins are perfectly acceptable—desirable, in fact for this type of party, and today they are available in all sorts of attractive patterns and colors. Avoid the dainty "would-be-china" patterns in favor of bold colors or checks. I like to use a mixture of bright solid colors—red, blue, olive green, and bright yellow—or the kind that simulate gingham checks. Then I pick up the colors in a big basket of mixed flowers set at one end of the kitchen counter—my "buffet table."

Lighting can be a problem in a kitchen, where the usual overhead light makes everyone look 10 years older. Counteract this by using just your stove light to cook by and supplementing it with lots of candles or, and this is what I use, kerosene lanterns.

They provide a real surprise when people come in, and everyone loves them.

For serving the 2 hot sauces, I use a pair of pretty enamelware double boilers, one red, the other yellow. But there are all sorts of handsome varieties on the market—the most luxurious, those wonderful copper ones with ceramic liners.

Everything except dessert service and coffee is set out on the longest kitchen counter—plates, napkins, accompaniments in their serving dishes, serving spoons and knives for spreading. Everyone assembles his own hamburger, helps himself to beer or Cokes, and gathers at the kitchen table, which I spread with a bold checked gingham cloth made from a few yards of dollar-a-yard gingham. For groups too large for a single table, I set up 2 card tables, but, as a word of warning, 8 to 10 people are about maximum for this type of party; over that, it's too hard to handle.

A big washtub filled with ice holds the beer and Cokes. I have painted mine bright yellow, and it never fails to amuse people. Coffee and dessert service is set out on a smaller side counter, and the party is on.

ABOUT BEEF FOR HAMBURGER

You will want fat-free ground round steak. Be definite with your butcher; don't just accept any ground beef or you may wind up with shrunken, tasteless patties that no one will enjoy. I tell my butcher I want lean top round of beef for steak tartare so he knows I really mean lean beef, not a mixture of beef and fat. Allow ½ pound meat for each guest; this makes 2 generous hamburgers. Have him grind it before your eyes and get it home as fast as you can. Now immediately mix it with other ingredients and shape into patties. Place each one on a piece of waxed paper, stack together, and store in your freezer.

An electric grill, big enough to cook 8 to 10 hamburgers at one time, is a real convenience, but if you don't own one or can't borrow one the hamburgers can be cooked equally well in the broiler.

About 1 hour before serving, brush the meat lightly with salad oil and let stand at room temperature until ready to cook. If you are using the broiler, turn it to high about 30 minutes before cooking the meat; it should be red hot.

ABOUT HAMBURGER ROLLS

Buy rolls at the same time you purchase the meat. Buy the best quality you can obtain; the few pennies extra for good firm rolls are well spent, for the cheaper varieties get "mushy" and disintegrate when the meat is placed on them. As soon as the meat is in the freezer, split the rolls and butter lightly; wrap securely in foil and freeze. About 1 hour before the party begins, place the open rolls on a baking sheet and toast lightly under a preheated broiler. Let the rolls remain on the baking sheet, covered with foil, ready to slide into a preheated oven for a few minutes of heating just before serving.

ABOUT GARNISHES

Lettuce can be prepared the day before and will still be crisp and fresh tasting. Boston lettuce has more taste and eye appeal, so try to use it if possible. Wash and shred the lettuce, wrap in wet paper towels, and store in the vegetable bin of your refrigerator. The wet paper towels somehow make the lettuce even crisper than when you started.

Sliced onions and tomatoes are fine on a hamburger, but *marinated* sliced onions and tomatoes are even finer, and they can be prepared ahead of time to great advantage. Allow at least 2 slices per guest. Arrange in a shallow serving dish and pour vinaigrette marinade over the slices. Cover tightly and refrigerate for at least 8 to 10 hours; longer is even better, so prepare them the night before if you like. Bring to room temperature before serving. The pickle relish, chutney, and crumbled cheese can be placed in serving dishes, covered with plastic wrap, and refrigerated until an hour or so before serving time.

The hot chili sauce and cheese rabbit can be made ahead and reheated or kept hot in double boilers. For this kind of party the double boilers are placed right on the serving counter, and guests help themselves right from the pots.

ABOUT DESSERT AND COFFEE

Apples taste best if crispy cold, so arrange the apple basket ahead of time also and refrigerate apples until just before serving. Incidentally, the cold makes the walnuts easier to crack. Even the cookies can be arranged in their serving dish or covered in the refrigerator until the last moment.

Since the peach mousse is frozen in individual molds, it needs only to be unwrapped and placed on serving dishes, complete with dessert spoons, already set out on a kitchen counter.

The coffee can also be made ahead. I prefer a glass or ceramic drip pot. Make the coffee about 1 hour before the party and keep it hot in a pan of just simmering water. Or use an automatic percolator that can be set to start at the right time. In either case, coffee cups, spoons, cream, and sugar are set out ready for guests to help themselves.

ABOUT COLD BEER AND COKES

Most cities have ice companies that will deliver party ice for a relatively small fee. Arrange to have it delivered about 1 or 2 hours before the party; large quantities of ice stay frozen a good long while. Fill the washtub with ice. Bury the beer and Cokes in it and place an opener and paper cups nearby.

That's all there is to it. Have a wonderful time!

◆

CHILI SAUCE

½ *pound beef chuck or round steak*
2 *tablespoons cooking oil*
1 *large onion, peeled and chopped*
2 *to 4 tablespoons chili powder*
1 *cup beef stock or broth*
3 *cups (3 8-ounce cans) enchilada sauce*
Salt

You can, of course, use ground beef, but for best flavor have your butcher mince the meat or do this job yourself. Buy the meat in one piece. Place it in the freezing compartment of your refrigerator until very firm, almost but not quite frozen. Use a chopping board and a very sharp knife and mince as finely as possible.

Heat the oil in a deep heavy skillet. Add the meat and cook, stirring, until no longer pink. Add the onion and continue to cook, stirring, until it is limp. Stir in chili powder; use more if you prefer. Then add stock and let simmer over low heat until liquid has evaporated and meat is tender, about 1 hour. Add enchilada sauce and cook, stirring frequently, for about 20 minutes, or until sauce is very hot and quite thick. Season with salt to taste.

MAKES ABOUT 4 CUPS.

◆

HOT CHEESE RABBIT

4 tablespoons butter
1 pound sharp processed cheese
1 cup beer or ale at room temperature
2 eggs
1 pound prepared Dijon or similar mustard
½ teaspoon Worcestershire sauce
Several dashes Tabasco sauce
½ teaspoon salt

Melt the butter in top half of a double boiler over simmering water. Add the cheese and stir until melted. Stir in ¾ cup of the beer (or ale) one tablespoon at a time, stirring well after each addition.

Beat the eggs with the mustard, Worcestershire sauce, Tabasco sauce and salt until blended and stir in remaining beer.

Add egg mixture to cheese mixture, stirring rapidly.

Keep rabbit hot over simmering water.

Serve from the pot.

MAKES ABOUT 3 CUPS.

◆

FROZEN PEACH MOUSSE

5 egg yolks
½ cup sugar
¼ cup cognac
6 large, ripe peaches
½ pint whipping cream

Beat the egg yolks with the sugar in the top half of a double boiler over simmering water until about triple in volume. Remove from heat and beat in cognac. Let stand at room temperature until cool. Peel, seed and mash the peaches to a smooth pulp and stir them into the cooled custard mixture.

Beat cream until stiff, fold in custard and pour into individual dessert molds. Cover each mold and freeze until firm.

Let stand at room temperature about 15 minutes before unmolding and serving.

SERVES 6.

◆

TEXAS SUMMERTIME OUTDOOR
SUPPER PARTY

THE MENU

Guacamole
Raw Vegetable Sticks
Corn Chips

Texas Red Hots

Beer

Red Hot Sauce   Chopped Onions
Pickle Relish
Grated Jack Cheese   Sauerkraut

Fresh Fruit Tarts
Coffee

For this Texas-Mexican menu, I use barn-red and sun-yellow flowered tablecloths and napkins, vivid background for Mexican peasant pottery in the same bold tones, plus edible centerpieces of radishes in small yellow bowls.

As this is a freewheeling, outsized, summertime party for a crowd, I set up several small buffet tables in different parts of the room instead of 1 large table, and I rent or borrow outdoor chairs and small tables to set out on the lawn and catch the overflow of guests.

Each buffet table is supplied with plates, napkins and forks, and a big yellow glass bowl of *guacamole* with another bowl of raw vegetable sticks and a straw basket of corn chips. A big red pot holds frankfurters, a chafing dish is filled with bubbly hot chili sauce, and another basket, napkin lined, holds the rolls. There are small yellow bowls of relish, onion, and cheese, and a second chafing dish for the sauerkraut.

Thick mugs and bottles of beer are on a nearby table in big tubs of crushed ice.

Everyone helps himself, of course, when and how he pleases, throughout the evening. The icy-cold light little fruit tarts and steaming hot coffee make a late appearance on a cart that is rolled out from the kitchen at just the right time.

ABOUT TEXAS RED HOTS

If you don't think of hot dogs as party food, think again. They are as gay as a carousel, as much fun as a circus, and can be as exciting as a day at the ball park. At the right time and in the right place nothing is so downright satisfying. What better time and place than a summer night at a country-style buffet party?

A Texas Red Hot is not just another name for a hot dog. It's a glorified version of a Dagwood. You start with a warm roll, add a frankfurter, then either red hot sauce or sauerkraut, or both if you are adventurous, plus chopped onion, relish, and grated cheese to fill the roll to its full capacity but not enough to make the creation unholdable.

Buy the best quality highly seasoned frankfurters available and serve them *hot*, really *hot*—lukewarm hot dogs are sorry fare. Quantity depends on the appetite of your guests, but for this menu I plan on 2 for each person, then add a few extra, just in case.

Put them in a large pot of water and bring to a full boil, then reduce heat and let simmer until ready to drain and serve. Bring to a full boil again just before serving. They can, of course, be kept hot in an electric skillet or chafing dish on the buffet table. If you do not have one, use a colorful red or blue enamelware pot to boil them; then, just before serving, drain off the water and bring to the table in the same pot. The heat from the pot will keep them hot for about half an hour.

As not everyone will want to serve himself at the same time, keep a second potful simmering on the stove to replace the first one when needed.

To serve 24 guests you will need:

48 to 60 frankfurters
48 to 60 frankfurter rolls
4 cups Texas Red Hot Sauce (recipe page 55)
3 or 4 large purple onions, peeled and chopped,
  or about 3 cups chopped onions
2 cups sour pickle relish
2 cups grated cheese
4 cups sauerkraut (recipe page 56)

ABOUT FRANKFURTER ROLLS

The rolls for Texas Red Hots should be "firm," as the sauce tends to make light and airy buns soggy. You'll usually find the type I mean in the freezer compartment at your supermarket, or get them fresh baked at your local bakery. Certainly, you'll want the best quality available.

ABOUT ONIONS

The best onions for eating raw are the big, mild and sweet purple variety, called Italian onions in some parts of the country. If these are not available, use small white ones; or peel and chop large yellow onions, put them in a nonmetal bowl, and cover with milk. Let soak for about an hour, then drain and blot thoroughly dry with paper toweling.

ABOUT RELISH AND CHEESE

Though any good brand can be used, a not too sweet relish is best. Buy firm, deep yellow, aged Monterey Jack cheese if you can find it. It's zesty but mellow and will melt just slightly when teamed with hot sauce. A good substitute is a New York or Canadian Cheddar.

ABOUT SAUERKRAUT

Buy the canned variety; unlike the raw kind in plastic bags, it has been cooked in the canning process. It takes less time to prepare and to my way of thinking has superior flavor. Prepare ahead and reheat.

ABOUT BEER

Because this is a party and just for fun, why not have an assortment of imported beers? Canada's light and lively Labatt Pilsener, pale golden Harp Lager from Ireland, bubbly Carta Blanca from Mexico, and smooth and creamy German Löwenbräu are just a few you'll find at today's supermarkets.

ABOUT COFFEE AND TARTS

How you prepare your coffee depends on your equipment, but do, when you serve it, serve it really hot, hot, hot! For this party I pour it from the pot into thick mugs. Sweeten each mug with a teaspoon of sugar (for those who want it) and add a cinnamon stick for stirring, which means no cream pitcher, sugar bowl, or spoons to bother about. I've yet to have a complaint.

The tarts taste best cold, so they remain refrigerated until just before serving. Each, in its own small foil tart pan, is placed on a paper napkin. And as they are only 2-bite size, I serve them, sans plate, as finger food.

◆

BORDER-STYLE GUACAMOLE
WITH RAW VEGETABLE STICKS AND CORN CHIPS

8 to 10 large avocados
4 to 6 large ripe but still firm tomatoes
1 large mild purple onion
½ cup freshly squeezed lemon juice
¾ to 1 cup Chili Sauce (recipe page 48)
½ teaspoon ground coriander (optional)
Tabasco
Salt
Raw vegetable sticks (description follows)
Corn chips

Don't trust to luck to find ripe avocados on the day of your party. Buy firm ones 2 or 3 days ahead and let them ripen at room temperature. Refrigerate only if they become really overripe before you are ready to use them.

Plunge tomatoes into boiling water, holding them in the water, one at a time, until the skins can be peeled off easily. Cut each into halves and gently squeeze out the seeds and juice. Then cut each half into thin strips. The strips must be free of seeds and juice or they will water down the *guacamole;* blot them dry if necessary with paper toweling. Put them in a small bowl, cover, and refrigerate until just before using. Peel the onion and mince very fine. Peel and seed the avocados; reserve the seeds. Place avocados in a large mixing bowl and mash with a fork. Add lemon juice and chili sauce. Season with coriander and Tabasco to taste. Fold in tomato strips and minced onion. Add salt to taste. Put the avocado seeds in the bowl until you are ready to serve the *guacamole.* They will prevent discoloration.

To serve, mound the *guacamole* in a large bowl. Place a smaller matching bowl of raw vegetable sticks on one side and a napkin-lined basket of corn chips on the other. Use a big wooden kitchen spoon for serving.

MAKES 24 SERVINGS.

NOTE: You may omit the chopped tomato and use 1 or more avocados in the *guacamole* if you prefer, as tomatoes are not a classic addition; however, they do "extend" the quantity (in season tomatoes are almost always inexpensive) and make this version more of a first-course salad than a cocktail dip.

RAW VEGETABLE STICKS

Use carrots, celery, turnips, zucchini in any combination. You will want about ⅓ cup vegetable slivers per person.

Scrape or peel as needed and cut into sticks as thin as possible and about 1½ inches long, or long enough to pick up with your fingers and dip into the *guacamole*. These are a nice alternate to the heavier corn chips and provide "salad" to give you a well-balanced menu.

◆

TEXAS RED HOT SAUCE

  2 tablespoons butter
  1 garlic clove, peeled and finely minced
  1 large yellow onion, peeled and finely chopped
  1 can (1 pound) barbecue-style beans
  1 can (8 ounces) tomato sauce
  ¼ cup bourbon whiskey or water
  2 tablespoons chili powder, or more
  2 or 3 dashes of Tabasco
  1 tablespoon Worcestershire sauce

Melt the butter in a large saucepan over medium heat. Add garlic and onion. Sauté until onion is limp. Place beans and tomato sauce in an electric blender. Add bourbon or water, chili powder, Tabasco, and Worcestershire. Cover and blend until smooth.

Pour into saucepan over sautéed onion and garlic. Heat to steamy hot. Serve with Texas Red Hots (frankfurters).

MAKES ABOUT 4 CUPS.

◆

SAUERKRAUT

3 tablespoons butter
1 large onion, peeled and finely chopped
1 large tart cooking apple, peeled and finely chopped
1 can (1 pound, 13 ounces) sauerkraut
2 tablespoons brown sugar
5 or 6 dashes of Tabasco
¼ cup water

Melt the butter in a large heavy saucepan. Add the onion and apple and cook, stirring often, until onion is limp and apple quite soft. Add the sauerkraut, brown sugar, Tabasco, and water. Stir to blend, then cook over low heat for about 1 hour, or until liquid has evaporated but sauerkraut is still moist. Keep hot or reheat.

MAKES ENOUGH FOR ABOUT 24 TEXAS RED HOTS.

◆

FRESH FRUIT TARTS

3 packages (3½ ounces each) vanilla pudding
    and pie filling
½ cup cognac or other good brandy
24 miniature baked tart shells
4 to 5 cups assorted fresh fruits (suggestions follow)
1 package (3 ounces) strawberry- or raspberry-
    flavored gelatin

Prepare pudding mix as directed on package but substitute the cognac or brandy for an equivalent amount of milk. Chill. Spoon into tart shells. Top with any of the fruits listed. Chill.

Meanwhile, prepare gelatin as directed on package. Chill until thickened. Spoon gelatin over tarts, using just enough to cover fruit with a smooth glaze. Chill until ready to serve.

MAKES 24 TARTS.

FRUITS
Sliced fresh peaches
Whole strawberries
Canned pineapple chunks, well drained
Fresh blueberries
Sliced bananas (sprinkle slices with fresh lemon juice
*   to prevent discoloration)*
Canned, or better yet fresh, pitted black cherries
Fresh seedless green grapes
Canned apricot halves, well drained

◆

SAUSAGE BUFFET

THE MENU

Pickled Beets   *Marinated Cucumbers*

Sausage Tray
Liverwurst
Blutwurst   *Paprika Salami*

Assorted Dark and Light Beers

Italian Pepperoni
Cervelat
Classic Potato Salad   *Macaroni and Bean Salad*

Thin-Sliced Rye
Pumpernickel
Crusty Round Italian Loaf
Long French Loaf

Escalloped Apples with Rum Pecan Cream Sauce
Coffee

What could be easier or more fun than a sausage buffet? The vegetables, salads, and dessert sauce can all be made 1 or 2 days ahead, the escalloped apples, conveniently prepared in frozen packages, need only be thawed and heated, and the rest of the menu is just a matter of intelligent and selective buying.

ABOUT SAUSAGES AND BREADS

All the sausages listed on this menu are meant only as suggestions, as are the breads. Buy both at the best delicatessen in town. Ask to taste each sausage before you buy—it's a great way to spend a lunch hour—then select the most interesting and varied assortment available. Don't have them sliced; buy smaller sausages whole, large ones by the pound in one piece. Choose breads not just for taste and texture but for eye appeal as well. Fat round Italian loaves, long skinny French ones, plump rye and pumpernickel. If you prefer, have the rye and pumpernickel sliced while you wait, but do leave some loaves whole to give interest and a marvelous still-life quality to your buffet table.

ABOUT SALADS

If this is a short-notice party and there just isn't time to make the potato and macaroni salads, buy them ready-made, then step up their bland flavors with a little judicious doctoring. Here's how to do it.

Dump your purchased salad into a large mixing bowl and add 1 or 2 tablespoons herb or wine vinegar or fresh lemon juice, plus a light sprinkling of any good seasoned salt. Toss gently until vinegar has been absorbed. Then taste; undoubtedly, the salad will still be undersalted. Add a little plain salt and then taste again. It's surprising how this one ingredient can improve even the most ordinary salad.

To embellish further, you can add 2 or 3 tablespoons minced chives and/or the same of minced parsley, plus a few pitted black or green olives, drained anchovies, or chopped sweet mixed pickles. If you have time, peel, core and chop, and toss in a tart apple. This last is one of my favorite taste boosters.

◆

PICKLED BEETS

2 cans (1 pound each) sliced beets
2 cups cider vinegar
6 cloves
2 tablespoons sugar
1 teaspoon salt
1 mild purple onion
Freshly ground black pepper
Lettuce

Drain beets. Place them in a large skillet and add vinegar, cloves, sugar, and salt. Bring to a full boil. Transfer to a long shallow nonmetal pan. Peel onion and slice as thinly as possible. Break slices into rings. Add to beets and mix gently with a fork. Sprinkle liberally with black pepper. Cover and refrigerate for several hours or overnight.

Drain and arrange on a lettuce-lined platter just before serving. MAKES 12 SERVINGS.

◆

MARINATED CUCUMBERS

6 large cucumbers
1 tablespoon salt
1 tablespoon sugar
½ cup vinegar
2 tablespoons salad oil
Black pepper
Lettuce
Chopped parsley (optional)

Peel the cucumbers. Cut lengthwise into halves and scoop out seeds. Slice as thinly as possible. Place in a nonmetal bowl and sprinkle with the salt. Toss with 2 forks to distribute salt evenly. Refrigerate for 1 hour or longer.

Drain thoroughly. Add sugar, vinegar, and oil. Toss to blend. Sprinkle with freshly ground black pepper. Serve from lettuce-lined bowl. Sprinkle with chopped parsley if desired.

MAKES 12 SERVINGS.

◆

ESCALLOPED APPLES
WITH
RUM PECAN CREAM SAUCE

4 packages (12 ounces each) frozen escalloped apples
Rum Pecan Cream Sauce (recipe follows)

Transfer frozen escalloped apples to a long shallow baking dish. Bake according to package directions. Serve warm from the dish. Serve cold sauce separately to spoon over each serving.

MAKES 12 SERVINGS.

RUM PECAN CREAM SAUCE
9 ounces cream cheese
3½ cups confectioners' sugar
½ cup cream
¼ cup light rum
Confectioners' sugar as needed
1 cup chopped pecans

Bring cream cheese to room temperature. Add 3½ cups confectioners' sugar and blend well. Heat cream to steamy hot. Add to cream cheese mixture and beat until smooth. Stir in rum. Add additional sugar as needed to bring the sauce to the consistency of heavy cream. Fold in nuts. Refrigerate. Transfer to serving bowl when well chilled and firm.

MAKES 12 SERVINGS.

Impromptu
Parties

◆

Most of the ideas in this book are for planned parties, but there is no reason why you can't cope with unexpected guests. With dessert ingredients such as plain cake layers, ice cream, frozen fruits, and sauces in your freezer, and with a small supply of party-special canned goods for appetizers, plus the recipes for half a dozen quick-cooking 1-skillet dishes, you can serve an unlimited variety of party meals.

Here are 2 weeknight menus that I frequently serve to out-of-town friends who arrive on the scene unexpectedly and are invited for dinner the same night.

In all cases ask your guests to arrive at 7:30 P.M. If you leave your job promptly at 5:00 this will give you 2½ hours for preparation. You do need that long, so be specific about the time. Plan your menu on your lunch hour or during your coffee break. If someone is at home, it's a good idea to call then and there to check the on-hand supplies. Next make a list of what you will need to complete your menu for quick shopping on the way home.

◆

IMPROMPTU DINNER ITALIAN-STYLE

THE MENU

Pimiento and Anchovy Salad
Italian Beef and Zucchini

Chianti

Crusty Italian Bread
Bel Paese Cheese
Fresh Pears   *Small Clusters of Purple Grapes*
Crisp Cookies
Coffee

The appetizer can be assembled from cans on your emergency party shelf. Chianti is the ideal wine for this meal, but another red wine will serve if it saves shopping time. The cookies, stored in airtight tins, can be kept on hand for just such an emergency.

Here are suggestions for timing:

5:00 to 5:30—Shop for groceries and wine on the way home.

5:30 to 6:45—Arrange cheese and fruit dessert on individual serving plates.

Grate the Parmesan cheese, then prepare the main dish. While this is cooking, arrange the appetizer course on individual small plates and refrigerate until time to serve. Make coffee.

Place cookies in napkin-lined basket.

Slice the bread and open the wine.

If you plan to serve drinks before the meal, set up a small bar in the living room.

Set the table.

6:45—The main dish, beef and zucchini, will be ready to take from the heat. Let stand covered at room temperature until time to reheat.

◆

ITALIAN BEEF AND ZUCCHINI

½ pound Parmesan cheese
1 large purple onion
6 to 8 small zucchini
2 large ripe tomatoes
2 tablespoons corn or safflower oil
1½ pounds top round of beef, ground
½ teaspoon salt
¼ teaspoon freshly ground black pepper

Grate the cheese. Place 1 cup of cheese in a serving bowl to pass at the table. Set aside remaining cheese (about 1 cup) to use in preparing the dish.

Peel and chop the onion. Cut zucchini into very thin slices. Coarsely chop the tomatoes. Heat the oil in a heavy skillet over medium heat. Add the beef and cook, stirring, until no longer pink. Add onion, zucchini, and tomato. Season with salt and pepper. Cover and cook over low heat for 25 to 30 minutes, or until zucchini is very soft. Stir frequently while mixture cooks. If it seems too dry, add 1 or 2 tablespoons water, but no more—the vegetables should provide the necessary liquid. Add the remaining cup cheese and stir it into the liquid. Cover and let stand at room temperature.

Reheat to steaming hot just before serving.

MAKES 4 GENEROUS SERVINGS.

NOTE: To extend the number of servings, cook 1 pound of flat noodles according to package directions and mix with beef and zucchini just before serving.

◆

IMPROMPTU DINNER FRENCH-STYLE

THE MENU

*Tomato and Orange Slices
with Parsley French Dressing*

Red Burgundy

*Tournedos and Flageolets
Crusty Hard Rolls
Coupe Tropicale*

Cointreau

Black Coffee

PARTY NOTES

5:00 to 5:30—Shop for groceries and wine on the way home.

5:30 to 6:45—Prepare salad. Prepare fruit for *coupe tropicale*. Chop chives and parsley.

Assemble all ingredients for *tournedos* and *flageolets* and place them near the skillet you plan to use for the cooking.

Arrange the *tournedos* on a plate, the chives and parsley in small bowls, and the bottled sauces, salt, pepper, and *flageolets* on a small tray, having first loosened all bottle tops. (I use my electric skillet and place it on a side table, in French chef fashion, along with all the ingredients and the entree plates for serving. This way I'm ready to cook when everyone is ready.)

Set the table. If you are going to serve drinks, set up your bar.

Arrange the rolls in a napkin-lined basket and open the wine.

7:30 to 8:00—Serve your guests a first drink or join them while they make their own.

Return to the kitchen, drain salad, place on salad plates, and bring to the table.

Assemble dessert.

Ask your guests to join you in the dining room or wherever you are going to cook and to bring their drinks with them while you prepare the entree.

Cook *tournedos* and *flageolets*. Turn skillet to very low while you and your guests enjoy the first course.

ABOUT FLAGEOLETS

Flageolets are small, pale green beans packed in jars or cans, imported from France and Belgium. They are admittedly expensive; however, they taste superb, with a mild but definite flavor unlike any other legume.

◆

TOMATO AND ORANGE SLICES
WITH PARSLEY FRENCH DRESSING

4 medium-sized ripe tomatoes
3 large oranges
Parsley French Dressing (recipe follows)

Plunge the tomatoes into boiling water until the skins can be peeled off easily. Cut each tomato into halves and gently squeeze out the seeds. Cut each half into thin slices.

Peel the oranges, removing as much of the white part of the peel as possible. Use a sharp knife; a long serrated professional chef's knife does the job neatly. With a small pointed knife push out any seeds from each slice.

Place tomato and orange slices in a long, shallow, nonmetal dish and pour the dressing over them. Let stand for 1 hour or longer before serving. Refrigerate if desired, but the flavor is best if the salad is served just slightly cold; overchilling dulls the flavor. Drain well before serving. Arrange in alternate rows of tomato and orange slices down the center of each salad plate.

MAKES 4 SERVINGS.

PARSLEY FRENCH DRESSING
¾ cup mild salad oil
¼ cup white-wine vinegar
2 tablespoons sugar
2 teaspoons salt
1 teaspoon pepper
½ cup minced parsley

Combine all ingredients except parsley in a small mixing bowl and beat with a wire whisk until thick. Add parsley and blend. Use as a dressing for any raw or cooked vegetables.

MAKES 1½ CUPS.

TOURNEDOS ET FLAGEOLETS

4 slices of beef fillet, cut ½ inch thick (tournedos)
2 teaspoons oil
1 tablespoon butter
2 tablespoons chopped chives
1 jar or can (1 pound) cooked flageolets
½ cup Escoffier Sauce Robert
1 tablespoon Worcestershire sauce
Coarse-ground black pepper
Salt
2 to 3 tablespoons minced parsley

Bring the *tournedos* to room temperature. This is important; if the center of the meat remains chilled the *tournedos* will not be juicy pink in the middle but bloody rare.

Heat the oil and butter in an electric skillet. Add the *tournedos* and cook them for about 3 minutes on each side. Add the chives and cook, stirring them gently, for a little less than 1 minute. Add the beans and all the liquid from the jar or can, the Sauce Robert, and Worcestershire. Stir to blend evenly with the beans. Season heavily with pepper and very lightly with salt. Let cook until beans are well heated and sauce is bubbly. Stir in parsley and serve at once.

MAKES 4 SERVINGS.

◆

COUPE TROPICALE

1 package (10 ounces) frozen raspberries
3 tablespoons Kirsch
1 large orange
1 large banana
8 small scoops of vanilla ice cream

Place frozen raspberries in a large mixing bowl. Add Kirsch. Break up frozen block as soon as it begins to thaw. Peel and section the orange; with a small pointed knife push out seeds from each section. Peel and slice the banana. Add fresh fruits to partially thawed raspberries and toss gently to blend.

If mixture is made more than 30 minutes before serving, refrigerate until almost time to serve. Raspberries should be almost thawed but still very cold.

Spoon some of the fruit and juice into 4 parfait glasses or, better yet, large brandy snifters. Cover with a scoop of ice cream. Repeat, ending with sauce.

MAKES 4 SERVINGS.

NOTE: The *coupe* can be put together at the last moment before you serve dinner. If stored in the refrigerator, the ice cream will remain firm for 30 to 45 minutes.

Entertaining
with
That Special
Drink

◆

A nice way to entertain inexpensively, but with style, is to have friends over for one very special, perfectly made drink before everyone, including yourself, goes on to a Saturday or Sunday brunch-lunch party. Of course, there's also the impromptu, but planned by you, "come for late drinks" after the show, concert, or dance.

According to Henri Delude who, as head barman, reigned over the elegant first-class Riviera Lounge aboard the S.S. *France*, drinks before noon should be completely different from cocktail-hour concoctions and different again from after-dinner imbibing. He advises that you select liquid refreshments that are congenial to the time of day. "No drink," he maintains, "should be pure stimulant. For entertaining drinks, think in terms not only of flavor but also visual pleasance. Just remember that the secret of a great drink is to keep it simple, as uncomplicated as possible."

◆

HENRI DELUDE'S RECIPES FOR MORNING DRINKS FOR BEFORE A BRUNCH-LUNCH

◆

BLOODY MARY

2 ounces good tomato juice
Juice from 1 small wedge of lemon
Dash of Tabasco
2 or 3 drops of Worcestershire sauce
Light sprinkling of celery salt
2 ounces vodka
Firm ice cubes

Mix in a double-sized old-fashioned glass. Add ice. Stir to chill. Serve at once.

MAKES 1 DRINK.

♦

BLOODY BULL

1 ounce good tomato juice
1 ounce beef consommé
Dash of Worcestershire sauce
Dash of Tabasco
Sprinkling of white pepper
2 ounces vodka
Firm ice cubes

Mix in a double-sized old-fashioned glass. Add ice. Stir to chill. Serve at once.

MAKES 1 DRINK.

♦

HENRI DELUDE'S
MIMOSA

3 ounces freshly squeezed orange juice
6 ounces dry Champagne

Chill both orange juice and Champagne. Serve in a stemmed 10-inch wineglass.

MAKES 1 DRINK.

◆

SCREWDRIVER

3 ounces freshly squeezed orange juice
2 ounces vodka
Ice cubes

Combine and serve on the rocks in a double-sized old-fashioned glass.

MAKES 1 DRINK.

◆

MY OWN
BLOODY MARY MIX FOR A CROWD
GIVEN TO ME BY HENRY COGGINS, WHO FIRST SERVED IT
AT A RECEPTION FOR GENERAL EISENHOWER.

Juice of 1 lime
1 can (1 quart) least expensive but reliable
brand of tomato juice
½ teaspoon monosodium glutamate (MSG)
1 tablespoon Worcestershire sauce
1 teaspoon Tabasco
1 quart inexpensive vodka, chilled

Roll the lime on the kitchen counter, using pressure, for a few seconds to obtain maximum juice. Mix juice with tomato juice and seasonings. Chill thoroughly. Add the vodka. Stir and serve over ice.

Henry maintains that it's the MSG plus lime juice that makes his Marys taste "expensive," i.e., very good.

MAKES 16 DRINKS.

◆

MY OWN
BUDGET SCREWDRIVER MIX

1 small can (6 ounces) frozen concentrated orange juice
Juice from 1 lime
1 bottle (10 ounces) club soda
1 quart inexpensive vodka, chilled

Mix first 3 ingredients and chill well. Add vodka. Serve on the
rocks.
MAKES 16 DRINKS.

◆

CHAMPAGNE WITH CASSIS

1 teaspoon Cassis, chilled
8 ounces dry Champagne, chilled

Place Cassis in a stemmed 10-inch balloon wineglass and swirl
until glass is coated evenly. Fill to brim with chilled Champagne.
MAKES 1 DRINK.

◆

DIETER'S MIMOSA

3 ounces freshly squeezed orange juice
6 ounces Perrier (nonalcoholic mineral water)

Refrigerate both orange juice and Perrier. Combine and serve
when well chilled.
MAKES 1 DRINK.

◆

DRINKS BEFORE LUNCH

THE PERFECT MARTINI

Like beauty, it's in the eye of the beholder. Cold it must be, dry it should be, but exact proportions of gin and vermouth will never be established to national satisfaction.

For me the perfect martini is 4 parts chilled English gin to 1 part chilled French vermouth. Pour into a chilled glass pitcher with plenty of large firm cubes of ice and stir gently for a few seconds only. Then strain into frosted, stemmed 2-ounce glasses. Twist a long thin slice of lemon peel over to extract 1 drop of oil essence; drop the peel in along with a small green olive.

◆

DAIQUIRI FOR TODAY PEOPLE

Half fill an electric blender with cracked, not crushed, ice. Add ½ teaspoon of superfine sugar for each jigger of freshly squeezed lime juice. For each jigger of lime juice add 4 jiggers of pale Jamaican rum. Blend at high speed for ½ second. Pour into chilled 4-ounce stemmed glasses.

◆

THE NEW MANHATTAN

It's dry, not sweet, and no longer lethal. Served on the rocks, it's what a very British friend calls a very civilized drink. Pour 2 parts blended whiskey and 1 part dry vermouth into an old-fashioned glass filled with large, firm ice cubes. Add an onion-stuffed green olive or not, as you prefer.

◆

MARGARITA PERFECTAMENTE

Fill 2 small bowls, 1 with coarse-ground sea salt, the other with lime juice. Chill 4-ounce stemmed glasses. Dip rims of glasses first into lime juice, then into salt.

For each drink mix together 2 ounces tequila, ½ ounce Triple Sec, and 1 ounce lime juice. Pour into an ice-filled old-fashioned cocktail shaker, shake, then strain into the salt-rimmed glasses.

◆

MIDAFTERNOON TO MIDNIGHT DRINKS

COME FOR CORDIALS AND CAKE

Today's replacement for an afternoon tea, a cordial and cake party is an especially good idea for any large gathering—for club, church, or political groups; to "meet the author" or a visiting politician; to honor a new member or "entertain the cast."

The committee will welcome the fact that there's no tea to brew and keep hot, no little sandwiches to make, no cream or sugar involved. Instead there's a dramatic, colorful, and elegant assortment of imported and domestic cordials and several types of homemade cake.

The cordials can be served in small chimney-shaped 5-ounce brandy glasses, in rounded 6-ounce sherry glasses, or over shaved ice in cocktail glasses (for the last, provide short straws).

The cakes should all be the dry varieties, sliced thin and cut into small squares. Ideal are poundcakes, fruitcakes, or nut breads, but any firm not-too-sweet cake that can be served as finger food will do nicely.

Save the dominant aromatic cordials such as Chartreuse, Benedictine, Crème de Menthe and Anisette for after-dinner imbibing. Serve instead velvety smooth and slightly sweet fruit liqueurs. These are the cordials best suited to afternoon.

COME FOR COFFEE AND LIQUEURS

"Come around nine for coffee and liqueurs." It's a party variation that's easy on the giver, delightful for the guests. There's time to unwind after work and eat a leisurely dinner at home.

Have lots of good hot coffee and a selection of liqueurs. Add a simple but superb poundcake sliced thin, or, if there's no time, buy really good bakery cookies—small crisp ones.

THE PERFECT AFTER-DINNER DRINKS

At the conclusion of the meal: a fine cognac or, if that's not affordable, a good brandy.

For 1 or 2 hours after dinner: a choice of liqueurs.

Later: a Crème de Menthe frappé (Crème de Menthe over shaved ice).

Much later: a stinger (2 parts cognac, 2 parts white Crème de Menthe, mixed and served over lots of shaved ice).

Later yet: a glass of cold fresh milk.

The
Sunday
Brunch-Lunch

◆

Styles change in entertaining fashions as well as in what we wear. High-noon Sunday brunch parties came on strong in the fifties, were all the go through the sixties, and are still with us, but their popularity is definitely on the wane. Our current self-indulgent society believes that on a day of rest one should rest, not spend the entire precious morning slaving over a hot stove.

Today it's the intimate little luncheon party that's the in thing. On Sunday it's a brunch-lunch with some foods faintly reminiscent of breakfast, but the hour has been changed to around 2 o'clock.

Ideally the meal should not take more than an hour to prepare, and the service should be leisurely, attuned to the day. The menu should be just a bit more special and different from that of the working week.

◆

AN INTIMATE TWO-COURSE BRUNCH-LUNCH

THE MENU

Choice of Aperitifs
Maryland Deviled Crab

California Sauvignon Blanc

Crisp Bacon
Danish Pastry ~~Surprise Muffins~~
or
Homemade Sweet Rolls
Tangerines
Coffee

This is a perfect lazy-day part-lunch, part-breakfast meal, taking altogether no more than 30 minutes to prepare. Scallop shells or individual ramekins of deviled crab are on the table before guests are seated, as is the dry white wine, a perfect accompaniment.

The second course, bacon, Danish or other pastry, and coffee, are on a side table. Buy the Danish pastry from a good bakery or bake your own homemade sweet rolls any time up to a month ahead (see pages 108–13 for the Day-Off-from-Work recipes). Kept warm on a hot tray, they can wait for guests to serve themselves.

For dessert there are tangerines and more coffee or perhaps a last sip of wine.

ABOUT CRABMEAT

Almost all crabmeat comes frozen these days, which for once doesn't change the flavor or quality of the product, but it must thaw, which takes at least 8 hours (for 1 pound) in your refrigerator. You can hasten the job at room temperature, but as crab is very perishable it's best to use it as soon as possible after it has thawed sufficiently to break up the frozen block. All packaged crabmeat, canned or frozen, has already been cooked.

ABOUT CRISP BACON

Place thick slices of bacon, not touching each other, in a long shallow pan. Place in a preheated 375° F. oven and let cook until almost done but not quite crisp. Remove from oven and let stand at room temperature until about 5 minutes before serving. Don't drain. Return pan to oven until bacon fat is lightly browned.

Remove from pan with a slotted spatula and drain on paper toweling.

◆

MARYLAND DEVILED CRAB

1 pound lump crabmeat
1 cup mayonnaise
½ cup Durkee Famous Sauce
½ cup commercially prepared croutons
1 tablespoon Dijon-style mustard
3 or 4 dashes of Tabasco
1 teaspoon Escoffier Sauce Diable or
    Worcestershire sauce
1 tablespoon lemon juice
Fine dry bread crumbs
Cold butter slivers, about 4 teaspoons butter

Preheat oven to 375° F.

Combine first 8 ingredients. Using 2 forks, mix gently but well. Divide the mixture evenly among 6 large or 8 small scallop shells or individual ramekins. Sprinkle each with bread crumbs, covering entire surface lightly with crumbs. Dot each with several butter slivers.

Bake for 15 to 20 minutes, or until crab is bubbly hot and crumbs are lightly browned.

MAKES 6 TO 8 SERVINGS.

◆

A PART-COOKOUT BRUNCH-LUNCH
ON THE TERRACE

THE MENU

Whiskey Sours

Sour-Cream Puffs

Panbroiled Steak with
Deviled Butter on Toast
or
Panfried Brook Trout
with Bacon

French Fried Onion Rings   Miniature Potato Cakes
Stuffed Baked Tomatoes

Bowl of Fresh Figs
or
Mixed Fresh Fruits
Coffee

Pecan Sweet Rolls
and
More Coffee

This part-cookout meal is both flexible and elastic. It's fun to plan and easy to give. All that's necessary is balmy weather, and even that can be dispensed with if you have a glass-enclosed terrace or porch. All recipes can be easily expanded, added to or doubled to accommodate the number of guests. Everything on the menu except the cookout food is quickly prepared in the kitchen to be kept hot or warm or cold as needed until time to bring out to wherever you set up your buffet table.

The steaks or trout can be panbroiled, the fish fried over or under any type of heat. Your equipment can be anything from a simple Japanese hibachi to a sophisticated electric grill or, with the help of big carrying baskets, you can transport everything out to your backyard barbecue fireplace.

If there's a fisherman in the family and the menu can feature his catch, the cost will be negligible for such party fare. But even if you decide to feature the steaks, the price of the entire meal will not be nearly as expensive as it looks and tastes.

ABOUT PANBROILED TROUT

If the trout was caught early in the morning on the day of your party consider yourself the most fortunate of cooks! But the mental strain is hardly worth it. Trout caught or bought 1 day ahead will do nicely. Have them cleaned or clean them yourself, leaving the heads and tails intact.

Mountain trout, speckled trout, or any small lake trout are the trout for panbroiling. As to the amount per serving, certainly you will need 1 6- to 8-inch fish for each person with extras for second servings. If they are smaller, you will want 2 or even 3 trout per guest.

ABOUT THE STEAKS

Ask your butcher for prime steaks from the rib eye, cut about ¼ inch thick. You won't find these in the ready-wrapped section of your supermarket; what is labeled there as sandwich steaks is rarely the same thing. Frankly, what you need here is a good butcher; the difference in price means a world of difference in flavor and tenderness. It doesn't pay to cut corners here; economize on other items or ask fewer guests, but don't try to save on the steaks. As for the amount you need, ½ pound for each person is a more than generous amount. This will work out to roughly 2 steaks per person, so that you can offer seconds.

About 1 hour before the party, arrange the raw steaks on an attractive platter, ring with parsley and lemon quarters, cover with plastic wrap, and bring to the cooking area. Meat must be at room temperature when it is cooked.

ABOUT DEVILED BUTTER

This should be soft and ready to spread on the just-cooked steaks. Use top-quality unsalted butter. Have the butter in an attractive crock right near the chafing dish, with a spreader handy to spread quickly on the still-sizzling steak.

ABOUT TOAST

Toast is toast, right? No, wrong! Toast used under steaks or fish can be a gooey mess or it can be crisp, crunchy, and delicious. Unfortunately, your faithful toaster can't really do the job. Base toast has to be baked in a slow 250° to 300° F. oven until almost crisp and just barely browned. This toast is perfect under steaks or fish; pan juices taste super delicious with crispy toast whereas if regular soft toast were used you would simply have mush. One word of caution—you must use the extra-thin-sliced, very firm bread for this; the soft doughy type of bread simply doesn't stand up.

ABOUT FRENCH FRIED ONION RINGS AND POTATO CAKES

Buy frozen onion rings; these separate into nice even rounds and need only to be heated in a moderate oven to crisp a bit before serving. Blot up excess grease by drying for a moment on paper towels before serving. They don't have to be oven hot, you know, just crisp. As for potato cakes, these also can be the frozen already-baked variety that only require thawing, heating, and crisping before arranging on the serving tray. I like to allow 1 10-ounce package for each 2 guests. They disappear like snow on a hot day, especially if there are male guests on hand. And what is a steak party without a few men around?

ABOUT FRESH FIGS

Admittedly, fresh figs are the ideal choice from the point of view of this Texas girl, but if they are not to be had or are just too expensive, happy substitutes include fresh Bing cherries, clusters of black and green grapes, tangerines, or crisp apples. The only real necessity is that the fruit be ripe, delicious, and beautiful. Pile it in a big silver bowl or a napkin-lined basket and let everyone help himself. And there you have it—everything you need to know for a super feast.

◆

SOUR-CREAM PUFFS

6 packages frozen patty shells
Sour cream
Currant jelly
Tabasco

Thaw frozen patty shells until soft but still cold. Roll out one at a time on a lightly-floured board as thin as possible. Roll from the middle, the thickest part of the patty shell. Trim off round edges to achieve an even square. Cut each square into 4 small pieces. Place about ¼ teaspoon sour cream and ¼ teaspoon currant jelly on each. Top jelly with 1 dash of Tabasco. Fold each square of dough over to form a small triangle. Prick top with the point of a sharp small knife. Arrange triangles on an ungreased baking sheet. Place in freezer until firm or until ready to bake.

Preheat oven to 400° F.

Bake the triangles until lightly puffed and lightly browned, about 10 minutes. Serve warm or cold.

MAKES 24 TINY PUFFS.

◆

PANBROILED STEAKS
WITH DEVILED BUTTER

12 rib eye steaks, cut ¼ to ½ inch thick
Deviled Butter (recipe follows)

Cut a little fat from each steak. You do not need much, just a piece about ½ inch long and about ¼ inch thick. Bring meat and fat to room temperature. Heat a 10-inch electric skillet to 500° F. (very hot).

Using a long-handled fork, rub the hot skillet with steak fat until the entire bottom is covered with a thin coating of rendered fat.

Put 2 steaks in the pan and sear them 30 seconds to 1 minute, or until the blood rises on the uncooked surface. Turn and sear the second side. Then continue to cook, turning often until done to taste—only a few seconds after searing both sides for rare, no more than 30 seconds after searing for medium-rare.

Spread each steak as it comes from the pan with deviled butter and serve at once.

MAKES 6 SERVINGS.

DEVILED BUTTER
½ *pound butter*
2 *tablespoons cognac*
½ *teaspoon salt*
½ *teaspoon coarse-ground black pepper*
1 *teaspoon Worcestershire sauce*
1 *tablespoon Escoffier Sauce Robert*
1 *teaspoon chili sauce*
½ *teaspoon Dijon-style mustard*

Bring butter to room temperature. Beat with a fork until light. Blend in cognac a little at a time. Add remaining ingredients and beat until blended. Cover and store in refrigerator if desired, but bring to room temperature before spreading on steaks.

MAKES ABOUT 1¼ CUPS.

◆

PANFRIED BROOK TROUT
WITH BACON

1 pound thick-sliced bacon
3 to 4 pounds pandressed brook trout
½ pound butter
Salt
Pepper
Paprika
Thin slices of lemon

In the kitchen broil or fry bacon until almost but not quite crisp. Drain on paper toweling, then wrap loosely in foil and seal. Set aside until ready to cook fish.

Cut each cleaned trout almost through lengthwise and spread open. Arrange trout on a large platter. Cover with foil or plastic wrap and refrigerate until ready to cook.

Reheat bacon over hot coals or in oven.

Melt butter in a large skillet over any type of medium-hot heat. When butter starts to sizzle, add 1 or 2 trout (depending on size) in a single layer, flesh side down. Fry for 2 or 3 minutes. Turn carefully with 1 or 2 spatulas and fry for 2 or 3 minutes longer.

Transfer to serving plate, flesh side up. Sprinkle with salt, pepper, and paprika. Place a piece of the hot cooked bacon on one side of fish, flip other side over it, closing fish. Top with slice of lemon and serve at once.

Fry remaining fish in the same manner.

MAKES 6 TO 8 SERVINGS.

◆

STUFFED TOMATOES

6 *small ripe but firm tomatoes*
Salt
¼ *pound butter*
1½ *cups packaged garlic-seasoned croutons*
1 *tablespoon steak sauce*
Chicken stock, if needed
Lemon pepper
Butter

Cut each tomato crosswise into halves. Squeeze each half very gently to remove seeds and juice. Use the handle of a teaspoon to remove any stubborn seeds. Sprinkle each cavity heavily with salt. Turn cut side down on paper toweling to drain for 15 to 30 minutes.

Melt the butter in a small skillet. Add the croutons and cook, stirring, over low heat until they soften. Add steak sauce and, if mixture seems too dry, 1 or 2 tablespoons of chicken stock. Season with lemon pepper. Fill each tomato with some of the mixture, packing it down. Arrange stuffed tomatoes side by side in a shallow baking dish. Top each with slivers of butter.

Bake in a preheated 350° F. oven for 25 to 30 minutes, or until the tomatoes are soft but not falling apart and the stuffing is lightly browned.

MAKES 6 SERVINGS.

◆

CITY WINTER BRUNCH-LUNCH

THE MENU

Dry Sherry

English Biscuits

Fresh Pineapple Quarters
with Black Grapes

Creamed Eggs Bombay-Style
Toast
Crisp Sugar-Glazed Bacon
Chutney

Applesauce Bread
Coffee

This menu can double nicely for a nonstuffy early-afternoon wedding reception, when everyone comes in church finery rather than casual clothes. The food is party pretty yet substantial enough to urge guests to "come hungry."

If it's a wedding, your table can be a still-life composition of sparkling glass and gleaming china on bare polished wood. Use your best silver, covered serving dishes for the eggs and bacon (mine are a matching pair), and a long silver tray (a tea tray doubles nicely) for the pineapple. An antique toast rack could complete the mood of an English hunt breakfast (not very expensive, and a wonderful addition to your party equipment) and the chutney in an oversized silver sugar bowl could add the final touch. All of the above party equipment can be rented if necessary.

Provide small hors d'oeuvre plates and forks for the first course, the pineapple, then large salad or small dinner plates for the hot food.

The applesauce bread, which is really more like a not-too-rich fruitcake, is cut into bite-sized squares and is passed with coffee as "finger food" after the used main-course plates have been whisked out of sight.

ABOUT SHERRY

There's a sherry to suit every occasion and every taste, from flint-dry, light-bodied Manzanilla to deep, rich, golden and sweet Cream. Obviously, buying sherry can be complicated, though it also can be direct and simple. To take the direct approach, which will get you home nicely; bear in mind the following:

Sherry is a blended, fortified wine, low in alcohol content (30 proof) and low (or lower than "hard" liquor) in calories. It's great for weight watchers but don't, for goodness sake, serve it for this reason alone. It's an acquired taste but once acquired can be enjoyed for a lifetime. Buy imported Spanish sherry, by brand name and by type. Though there are good domestic sherries on the market, not one of them tastes quite like the original. None, to my mind, has that same earthy taste of the soil and the sun of Spain.

For this menu serve *fino* dry sherry, at room temperature or just slightly chilled, in stemmed glasses with a bowl about 4 inches high, filling them only about half full. Or use highball glasses with half soda and plenty of ice or serve on the rocks in old-fashioned glasses. The first way is classic Spanish, and to be absolutely correct the glass should be larger at the bottom of the bowl than at the top so that each time it is lifted the aroma and fragrance can be enjoyed before sipping the wine. The other ways are "American modern" and currently fashionable, lovely and light, but it's really a matter of choice.

ABOUT FRESH PINEAPPLE

To test for ripeness put the pineapple close to your nose and inhale. What you should get is a sunny, decidedly pineapple fragrance. Pull on a leaf near the top. It should come away with just a little resistance; too easily means the fruit might be past its prime. Finally, thump first the inner side of your wrist, then the pineapple. If the sounds are the same, the fruit should be of the best, ripe but not too ripe.

ABOUT BACON

For the greatest bacon you have ever tasted, buy top-quality slab bacon and have your butcher slice it thick. How thick? Tell him you want no more than 10 or 12 slices to the pound. If you can find it, buy the American version of Irish bacon; it's usually lean, with good flavor.

ABOUT CHUTNEY

Buy Major Grey type; imported English chutney is, to my mind, the best. If you can persuade your Florida-bound friends to bring ripe mangoes back with them, and if you have a morning to spare, make your own. It's easy, never-fail, and fun. It will cost, per pint jar, about a quarter of the price of commercially made, and it will taste delicious (recipe page 95).

ABOUT APPLESAUCE CAKE

Make ahead when you are in the mood (recipe page 220). Freeze until you need just such a bread to serve with coffee or tea, or anytime.

◆

FRESH PINEAPPLE QUARTERS
WITH BLACK GRAPES

2 small ripe pineapples
Cointreau or Kirsch liqueur (optional)
1 pound large black grapes, approximately

Leaving pineapple "greenery" attached, cut each pineapple lengthwise into halves, then cut each half lengthwise, making a total of 8 quarter wedges. With a sharp knife, start at the end of each wedge and cut the fruit as closely as possible away from the peel in one long piece. Cut fruit across into bite-sized pieces. Then carefully reassemble the pieces of fruit in the peel. If desired, sprinkle lightly with liqueur. Using multicolored wooden food picks, spear 1 grape into each piece of fruit, making a row of grapes down the center. Refrigerate until time to serve.

MAKES 8 SERVINGS.

◆

CREAMED EGGS BOMBAY-STYLE

2 cups chicken stock or broth, canned
   or homemade (recipe pages 185–86)
1 celery rib, coarsely chopped
2 garlic cloves, peeled and cut into halves
2 small white onions, peeled and quartered
1 small tomato, chopped
1 bay leaf
Salt
4 tablespoons butter
2 tablespoons curry powder
2 tablespoons flour
1 cup light cream
2 tablespoons applesauce
6 to 8 hard-cooked eggs, sliced
Toast points

Combine chicken stock or broth, celery, garlic, onions, tomato, and bay leaf in a saucepan. Season lightly with salt. Let simmer over low heat until reduced by half, about 30 minutes. Strain and set aside.

Melt the butter in a second saucepan over moderate heat. Stir in the curry powder and cook, stirring, for a few moments; then stir in the flour and continue to cook and stir for a full 3 minutes. Remove from heat and slowly add the strained chicken stock, stirring as it is added. Return to heat and add the cream and applesauce. Cook and stir until thick and smooth. Correct seasoning with salt.

If sauce is made ahead, cover directly with plastic wrap to keep film from forming. Store in refrigerator.

When ready to proceed bring sauce to room temperature, then reheat to steamy hot. Do not allow to boil. Arrange hard-cooked egg slices in an attractive shallow oval baking dish. Cover with sauce. Place in a preheated 350° F. oven and let bake for 5 minutes. Serve from the dish, over crisp toast points.

MAKES 6 TO 8 SERVINGS.

◆

CRISP SUGAR-GLAZED BACON

1½ pounds slab bacon
2 tablespoons brown sugar

Have your butcher slice the bacon into 18 to 20 thick slices. Place bacon slices in a single layer, not touching each other, in a long shallow baking dish. Place in a cold oven. Turn heat to 300° F. and bake until crisp. Sprinkle with sugar about 3 minutes before taking from oven. Drain on paper toweling.

Serve immediately, or undercook slightly, wrap in foil until ready to serve, and reheat in a preheated 350° F. oven.

MAKES 6 TO 8 SERVINGS.

◆

MANGO CHUTNEY
A DAY-OFF-FROM-WORK RECIPE

4 large mangoes, about 4 cups peeled and sliced
1 large mild purple onion
4 small hot peppers
1 garlic clove
1 pound light brown sugar
1 cup apple-cider vinegar
2 teaspoons salt
1 jar (8 ounces) preserved ginger in syrup
1 pound seedless raisins
1 cinnamon stick (1 inch), broken up

Peel and slice mangoes. Peel and chop fine the onion, peppers, and garlic. Place in a large preserving kettle. Add sugar, vinegar, salt, and syrup from ginger. Chop ginger to coarse pieces and add to preserving kettle. Add raisins and cinnamon. Bring to a boil, then reduce heat and let simmer for about 1 hour.

Remove from heat and let cool to room temperature for several hours, or cool, then refrigerate and proceed the next day. Bring to a boil a second time. Reduce heat and let simmer for about 30 minutes. Ladle into hot just-scrubbed and well-rinsed jars and seal.

MAKES ABOUT 5½ PINTS.

•

CALIFORNIA SUNSHINE BRUNCH-LUNCH

THE MENU

Champagne and Orange Juice

Cinnamon Sugar Puffs

*California Deviled Chicken
with Pineapple*

*Stuffed and Broiled
Mushrooms*

Coffee

ABOUT BUYING MUSHROOMS

Buy extra-large, very fresh young mushrooms. Though large and young may sound like contradictions, in this case they are not. Unlike the situation with vegetables or fruits, the size of a mushroom is no indication of its age or quality. Large or small, really fresh mushrooms are smooth, chalky white, and unblemished, with no space between the inverted rim of the caps and stems. Too long in the market, their moisture evaporates and the caps open, showing on the undersides a velvety ring of miniature pleats that change in color as the mushroom ages from pale beige to dark brown.

ABOUT STUFFED AND BROILED MUSHROOMS

You can prepare the stuffing 1 day ahead, but the mushrooms taste best if they are left in an airtight package in the refrigerator until the day you serve them. To avoid last-minute work, they can be stuffed 2 or 3 hours before broiling. Arrange them on the broiler tray and cover the tray with plastic wrap. Store in the refrigerator until time to bake. Served hot from the oven, they will stay warm enough to eat for about 1 hour.

ABOUT CALIFORNIA DEVILED CHICKEN WITH PINEAPPLE

You can substitute leftover turkey for the chicken, or, if there is not enough, you can add top-quality canned chicken meat, or use all canned chicken meat and canned chicken stock, or cook your own chicken and make your own stock several days ahead of the party (recipe page 99).

When all ingredients are prepared and lined up near the cooking pot, the dish takes no more than 20 to 25 minutes to make. It can be prepared ahead and reheated or kept hot until time to serve.

ABOUT CHAMPAGNE AND ORANGE JUICE

As this is a midday party and the Champagne is to be served half and half with orange juice, 2 bottles should be ample to serve 8 guests. You don't have to be an expert on wine to buy Champagne. The only problem is the price; unless you are extremely knowledgeable, a vintage Champagne is not worth the extra 3 or 4 dollars it costs over nonvintage. As the Champagne for this party is to be mixed with juice, you don't need an expensive French import. Buy *brut* (very dry) or *extra sec* (fairly dry), and buy by the brand name. My choice for this menu: California Almaden Blanc de Blancs.

Champagne should be served chilled but not icy cold. Chill the orange juice as well but don't dilute either one with ice. Mix just before serving. Serve any other wine "on the rocks" but please, never Champagne.

◆

BAKED STUFFED MUSHROOMS

12 large fresh mushrooms
2 tablespoons butter
¼ cup finely chopped scallions
2 tablespoons dry Madeira
1 cup finely minced, lean baked ham
Heavy cream
Salt
Pepper
1 tablespoon grated Parmesan cheese
Butter slivers

Remove stems from mushroom caps, trim off ends and chop as finely as possible.

Melt the butter in a small skillet. Add chopped mushroom stems and scallions. Cook over low heat until very soft. Add Madeira, increase heat and stir until liquid has evaporated. Remove from heat and stir in ham. Add sufficient cream (a tablespoon at a time) to hold mixture together. Season with salt and pepper. Fill mushroom caps with mixture and sprinkle each lightly with Parmesan cheese. Dot each with small slivers of butter and place them in a shallow baking dish just large enough to hold them compactly.

Bake in a preheated 350° F. oven until caps are tender and filling lightly browned—about 15 minutes.

MAKES 6 SERVINGS.

◆

CALIFORNIA DEVILED CHICKEN
WITH PINEAPPLE

4 tablespoons butter
4 tablespoons flour
2 cups chicken stock or broth, canned or homemade
1 cup milk
1 can (2¼ ounces) deviled ham
2 or 3 dashes of Tabasco
1 teaspoon Worcestershire sauce
½ teaspoon A1 sauce
Coarse-ground black pepper
Salt
4 cups large bite-sized pieces of cooked chicken
*   or turkey*
8 slices of canned pineapple, well drained
Butter slivers
8 slices of thin white bread

Melt the butter in a large heavy saucepan and stir in the flour.
Cook briefly, stirring with a wooden spoon. Remove pan from
heat and slowly add the stock and milk, stirring as it is added.
When blended, cook over moderate heat, stirring often, until
mixture begins to thicken. Add the deviled ham and stir until
thoroughly blended. Add seasonings to taste and chicken and
continue to cook until chicken is heated and sauce is thick and
smooth.

Cut each slice of pineapple into halves, place on foil, and dot
with slivers of butter. Place under broiler and heat until butter
has melted. Add to deviled chicken just before serving.

Remove crusts from bread slices and cut each slice diagonally
into halves. Toast lightly.

To serve, transfer chicken, pineapple, and sauce to a chafing
dish or electric skillet. Bring to the buffet table and keep warm
until time to serve. Serve over toast points.

MAKES 8 SERVINGS.

◆

CINNAMON SUGAR PUFFS

½ cup sugar
1 tablespoon ground cinnamon
3 frozen patty shells

This is a super-easy recipe.

Combine sugar and cinnamon. Thaw patty shells until soft but still cold. Place on a lightly floured board and roll out to a thickness of about ⅛ inch. Sprinkle with sugar and cinnamon mixture. With a sharp knife cut into strips about ½ inch long and ¼ inch wide. Place strips, not touching, on a baking sheet. Place baking sheet in freezer and refreeze strips until firm.

Meanwhile heat oven to 400° F.

Place frozen strips on a cold baking sheet and bake until puffed and lightly browned, about 10 minutes. Serve hot or cold.

MAKES ABOUT 24 STRIPS.

Breakfast
to End
the Evening

◆

One of the happiest, easiest ways to entertain (at least for me) is to invite people for breakfast to end the evening—after the theater or even after the movies. I hasten to add that this type of party is best limited to Friday or Saturday night, but when there's a long, leisurely day ahead why not make a night of it? Make it a kitchen party. People are in a relaxed, happy mood after a pleasant evening, so let your guests help with last-minute chores while you finish the main-course dish.

The 2 menus here are my favorites. They are both extra easy, both lend themselves to preparing ahead, and both are successful in that they always please everyone.

For the first, the grapefruit tastes even better for being prepared ahead and left in the refrigerator to absorb the flavor of the Kirsch. The corned-beef hash can be ready and waiting in the baking dishes. Cover with aluminum foil and leave at room temperature for an easy, fast finish. Have the eggs nearby in a handy bowl. When you arrive home you need only turn on the oven, break the eggs into the indentations in the hash, re-cover with foil, and bake. The rolls can be buttered and left at room temperature in a foil-covered pan. The coffee should be measured and in the pot, needing only water and heat to bring to fragrant perfection.

The second menu is equally simple even though it does sound like a bit more doing. The *frittata* can be prepared ahead right to the point where you add the eggs, covered with foil, and left until you are ready to beat the room-temperature eggs and complete the dish, a matter of 5 minutes at the outside.

The garlic bread can be left foil-wrapped, ready to heat in the oven along with the doughnuts. And to my mind the longer you let the apples stand around absorbing the cognac the better.

One final and pleasant note about late breakfast parties—they are gay, taste marvelous, and make only slight inroads on the paycheck. Have drinks available if you like, but the fragrance of freshly brewed coffee along with the aroma of eggs and breads quickly lures most anyone away from the last nightcap of the evening. How else could you build a party reputation with less money and work?

◆

SATURDAY BREAKFAST TO END THE EVENING ✓

THE MENU

Grapefruit with Kirsch

Corned-Beef Hash and Shirred Eggs
Basket of Hot Rolls

Coffee

◆

CORNED-BEEF HASH AND SHIRRED EGGS

4 tablespoons butter
4 small white onions, peeled and finely chopped
4 celery ribs, finely chopped
1 small green pepper, seeded and finely chopped
3 cans (1 pound each) corned-beef hash
4 dashes of Tabasco
1 tablespoon Worcestershire sauce
½ teaspoon coarse-ground black pepper
Salt
8 eggs
Chopped parsley

Melt the butter in a large heavy skillet and add the onions,

celery, and green pepper. Sauté over medium heat until vegetables are limp. Add the hash and break it up with the tip of a
spatula. Cook, stirring often, until mixture is well blended and
hash is hot. Stir in the seasoning. Blend and cook over low heat
for about 15 minutes. Stir often and turn hash over as it cooks.
Transfer hash to 2 baking dishes, each 6 x 10 x 12 inches. Spread
out to cover the bottom of the pans evenly and completely. Set
aside until ready to bake.

Preheat oven to 375° F.

Using the back of a large spoon, make 8 shallow indentations
in the surface of hash. Break each egg into a saucer, then gently
pour it into an indentation. Cover baking dishes with foil and
seal. Place on the middle rack of oven and bake until whites of
eggs have set. Yolks will be soft but not runny. Sprinkle with
chopped parsley. Serve from the baking dishes.

MAKES 8 SERVINGS.

◆

SATURDAY BREAKFAST TO END THE EVENING

THE MENU

Skillet Apples
Frittata
Garlic Bread

Doughnuts
Coffee

◆

FRITTATA

1 tablespoon butter
1 tablespoon mild cooking oil
4 green onions, minced
2 medium-sized cold boiled new potatoes,
  coarsely chopped
½ to ¾ cup leftover cooked green peas, well drained,
  or substitute chopped cooked zucchini,
  green beans, or spinach
1 tablespoon chopped pimiento (optional)
4 large eggs
⅓ teaspoon salt
Sprinkling of freshly ground black pepper
Dash of Tabasco (optional)
1 tablespoon grated Parmesan cheese

Adjust broiler rack to about 6 inches below source of heat.
Preheat broiler to 500° F.

Melt butter with oil in a heavy 9- or 10-inch ceramic-coated cast-iron skillet over medium heat. Add onions and sauté until limp. Add potatoes and cook until heated thoroughly. Use a spatula to turn and stir often as they heat. Stir in peas and pimiento. Spread potatoes and vegetables evenly over bottom of skillet.

Beat eggs with salt, pepper, Tabasco, and Parmesan cheese until blended, then pour over potato mixture, tilting skillet back and forth to distribute egg mixture evenly. Do not stir. Cook only until eggs at bottom of skillet have set.

Transfer skillet to preheated broiler oven until the *frittata* is firm and the surface lightly browned. Cut into pie-shaped wedges. Lift wedges from skillet with a spatula onto warm serving plates and serve at once.

MAKES 4 SERVINGS.

◆

SKILLET APPLES

4 to 6 large crisp apples
1 cup sugar
1 cup water
¼ cup cognac, brandy, or light rum

Core the apples and peel the top third of each. Place sugar, water, and apple peelings in a large shallow skillet. Stir over medium heat until sugar dissolves. Let simmer for about 10 minutes. Add the apples, cover, and let cook over low heat, turning them often until apples are tender but not falling apart.

Transfer apples to a serving bowl. Remove peelings from syrup and discard. Add cognac to syrup and bring to a full boil; remove from heat and cool to lukewarm. Pour over apples. Baste apples with syrup for 1 or 2 minutes.

Serve warm, or refrigerate for several hours and serve very cold.

MAKES 4 TO 6 SERVINGS.

Open-House Coffee

◆

ON THE FRESH FRUIT BUFFET TABLE

Platter of Honeydew Melon Slices
with Lime Wedges

Big Bowl of Fresh Strawberries
with a Bowl of Brown Sugar
and a Bowl of Sour Cream

Platter of Thick Orange Slices
with Powdered Sugar
and Chopped Mint

ON THE COFFEE BUFFET TABLE

Big Straw Baskets of Warm Homemade Rolls
(Bowknots, Crisp Rolls, Pecan Sticky Buns)
Whipped Cream Cheese
with Orange Marmalade
Butter   Strawberry Jam
Hot Coffee   Iced Coffee

◆

BREAKFAST BOWKNOTS
A DAY-OFF-FROM-WORK RECIPE

3¾ to 4¼ cups unsifted all-purpose flour
½ cup sugar
2 teaspoons salt
2 packages active dry yeast
¾ cup milk
½ cup water
¼ pound butter
1 egg, at room temperature
Crumb Topping (recipe follows)
Melted butter

These can be made up to 1 week in advance.

In a large bowl thoroughly mix 1½ cups flour, the sugar, salt, and yeast.

Combine milk, water, and ¼ pound butter in a saucepan. Heat over low heat until liquids are very warm (120° to 130° F.). Gradually add to dry ingredients and beat at medium speed of electric mixer for 2 minutes, scraping bowl occasionally. Add egg and ½ cup flour. Beat at high speed for 2 minutes, scraping bowl occasionally. Stir in enough additional flour to make a stiff batter. Cover bowl tightly with aluminum foil. Refrigerate for 2 to 24 hours.

Prepare crumb topping. Turn dough out onto a lightly floured board; divide into halves. Roll each half to a rectangle 15 x 8 inches. Cut into 15 strips 1 inch wide. Loosely tie each strip into a knot, leaving a loose loop in center. Place on greased baking sheets. Brush knots with melted butter. Sprinkle with prepared crumb topping. Let rise uncovered in a warm place free from draft until doubled in bulk, about 1 hour.

Bake at 250° F. for 30 minutes. Remove from baking sheets and cool on wire racks. Wrap in plastic bags. Store in refrigerator for up to 7 days.

When ready to serve, place on ungreased baking sheets. Bake at 400° F. for 6 to 8 minutes, or until browned. Remove from baking sheets and cool on wire racks.

MAKES 30 ROLLS.

CRUMB TOPPING

Mix together ⅓ cup unsifted flour, ⅓ cup firmly packed dark brown sugar, 1 teaspoon ground cinnamon, and 2 tablespoons softened butter until mixture is crumbly.

REFRIGERATOR ROLLS
A DAY-OFF-FROM-WORK RECIPE

5 to 7 cups unsifted all-purpose flour
½ cup sugar
4 teaspoons salt
2 packages active dry yeast
1½ cups milk
1½ cups water
¼ pound butter

These can be made up to 1 week in advance.

In a large bowl thoroughly mix 3 cups flour, the sugar, salt, and yeast. Combine milk, water, and butter in a saucepan. Heat over low heat until liquids are very warm (120° to 130° F.). Gradually add to dry ingredients and beat at medium speed of electric mixer for 2 minutes, scraping bowl occasionally. Add 2 cups flour. Beat at high speed for 2 minutes, scraping occasionally. Stir in enough additional flour to make a soft dough. Turn out onto a lightly floured board; knead until smooth and elastic, about 8 to 10 minutes. Place in a greased bowl, turning to grease top. Cover; let rise in a warm place free from draft until doubled in bulk, about 1 hour.

Punch dough down; turn out onto a lightly floured board. Divide dough into 4 equal pieces. Divide each piece into 12 equal pieces. Shape each piece into a smooth round ball. Place in large greased muffin cups, 2½ x 1¼ inches. Cover and let rise in a warm place free from draft until almost doubled in bulk, about 45 minutes.

Bake at 275° F. for 20 to 25 minutes, or until rolls just start to change color. Cool in pans or on sheets for 20 minutes. Remove from pans or sheets and finish cooling on wire racks. Wrap tightly in plastic bags and refrigerate for up to 7 days.

Just before serving, place rolls on an ungreased baking sheet.

Bake at 400° F. for 10 to 12 minutes, or until golden brown. If desired, brush with melted butter.

MAKES 48 ROLLS.

◆

FREEZER ROLLS
A DAY-OFF-FROM-WORK RECIPE

5½ to 6½ cups unsifted all-purpose flour
½ cup sugar
1½ teaspoons salt
2 packages active dry yeast
1¼ cups water
½ cup milk
¼ pound butter
2 eggs, at room temperature

These can be made up to 4 weeks in advance.

In a large bowl thoroughly mix 2 cups flour, the sugar, salt, and yeast. Combine water, milk, and butter in a saucepan. Heat over low heat until liquids are very warm (120° to 130° F.). Gradually add to dry ingredients and beat at medium speed of electric mixer for 2 minutes, scraping bowl occasionally. Add eggs and ½ cup flour. Beat at high speed for 2 minutes, scraping bowl occasionally. Stir in enough additional flour to make a soft dough. Turn out onto a lightly floured board; knead until smooth and elastic, about 8 to 10 minutes. Cover with plastic wrap, then with a towel, let rest for 20 minutes.

Punch dough down. Shape into small balls. Place on greased baking sheets. Cover with plastic wrap and foil, sealing well. Freeze until firm. Transfer to plastic bags. Freeze for up to 4 weeks.

Remove from freezer; place on greased baking sheets. Cover

and let rise in a warm place free from draft until doubled in bulk, about 1½ hours.

Bake at 350° F. for 15 minutes, or until golden brown and done. Remove from baking sheets and cool on wire racks.

MAKES ABOUT 45 ROLLS.

◆

PECAN STICKY BUNS
A DAY-OFF-FROM-WORK RECIPE

5½ to 6½ cups unsifted all-purpose flour
¾ cup sugar
1 teaspoon salt
3 packages active dry yeast
¼ pound butter, at room temperature
1 cup very warm tap water (120° to 130° F.)
3 eggs, at room temperature
Melted butter
½ cup firmly packed dark brown sugar

These can be made up to 4 weeks in advance.

Prepare pans (directions follow). Set aside until ready to use.

In a large bowl thoroughly mix 1¼ cups flour, the sugar, salt, and yeast. Add butter. Gradually add tap water to dry ingredients and beat at medium speed of electric mixer for 2 minutes, scraping bowl occasionally. Add eggs and ¼ cup flour. Beat at high speed for 2 minutes, scraping bowl occasionally. Stir in enough additional flour to make a soft dough. Turn out onto a lightly floured board; knead until smooth and elastic, about 8 to 10 minutes.

Divide dough into halves. Roll out one half to a rectangle 14 x 9 inches. Brush with melted butter and sprinkle with half of the brown sugar. Roll up from short end to form a roll 9 inches long. Pinch seam to seal. Cut into 9 1-inch slices. Arrange slices cut side up in a prepared pan. Cover pan tightly with plastic wrap, then with aluminum foil; place in freezer. Repeat with remaining dough and sugar. Keep frozen for up to 4 weeks.

Remove from freezer. Let stand, covered with plastic wrap, at room temperature until fully thawed, about 3 hours. Remove plastic wrap, cover lightly, and let rise in a warm place free from draft until more than doubled in bulk, about 1 hour and 15 minutes.

Bake at 375° F. for 20 to 25 minutes, or until done. Cool in the pan for 10 minutes. Invert rolls onto plates to cool.

MAKES 18 ROLLS.

TO PREPARE PANS

Melt ¼ pound butter. Stir in 1 cup firmly packed dark brown sugar and ½ cup light corn syrup. Heat, stirring, until sugar is dissolved. Pour into 2 greased 9-inch-square pans. Sprinkle each pan with ½ cup broken pecans.

The
Perfect
Buffet
Dinner

◆

As I see it, a buffet table should look positively crowded with good things to eat, no matter if it is or not. Two small well-laden tables are better than a single large one with too many empty spaces between the dishes.

When selecting a buffet menu think of what serving platters, bowls, and casseroles you will use, then visualize how they can be arranged on the table. Everything should combine to look, as well as taste, great together.

Buffet food should have "staying power." Nothing looks less attractive than an aspic running to soup or a green salad wilted from waiting.

Have "extras" ready in the kitchen to refill half-empty platters and replace empty casseroles. Nothing is quite as dreary as a half-eaten feast.

Guests should be able to serve themselves easily; I have yet to see anyone at a buffet meal who likes to carve his own serving of ham or turkey. Also, unless everyone can proceed from the buffet to a completely set dining table, it's essential to stay with food that can be eaten with one hand. It's just not possible for anyone perched on the edge of a sofa with a plate on the coffee table to manage both a knife and fork.

Here are some pointers to help you save yourself.

SELECT THE RIGHT MENU

If you have time you can prepare everything—well, almost everything—for a party meal ahead. This means less tension for most people, but the truth is that, unless you plan carefully, it can also be more work—usually after-work work, and that to me is the worst kind.

If you select a menu with all complicated, time-consuming recipes, you may find it necessary to spend every night after work in the kitchen for a week before your party as well as devote several lunch hours to shopping for ingredients. And you'll still have quite a bit of work, reheating and assembling, to attend to on the day of the party.

If, on the other hand, you balance the meal with at least half quick and easy dishes—for example, a hearty casserole, an easy-to-make salad, and a meat platter using delicatessen meat, you can prepare the entire menu ahead or not, in 2 or 3 hours total.

THINK BEFORE YOU SHOP

Plan your menu, then with written recipes in hand write out a detailed grocery shopping list—not by ingredients as listed in the recipes but under supermarket sections and other shops. List *all* ingredients; then before you leave the house, "shop" your kitchen and cross off "on hand" supplies. Here's an example.

THE MENU

Pâté Louise
Water Biscuits
(*on the coffee table*)

Scotch and
Vodka Sours
or with Soda

Dry Red Wine

Platter of Jellied Sour-Cream Coleslaw
with Scandinavian Beet Salad
and Green Asparagus Vinaigrette
Riso al Modo di Gauchos
Cold Roast Beef Platter

Tipsy Ice-Cream Pie

Spanish Brandy

Demitasse

SHOPPING LIST

At the supermarket

DAIRY INGREDIENTS
Sour cream: 1 1-pint carton
Butter: 1 pound
Eggs: on hand
Heavy cream: ½ pint

CANNED AND BOTTLED INGREDIENTS
3 packages (3 ounces each) lemon-flavored gelatin
1 package unflavored gelatin: on hand
Apple-cider vinegar: on hand
Mayonnaise: 1-quart jar of firm real mayonnaise
1 can (1 pound) sliced beets
1 can (1 pound) green asparagus
Safflower oil: on hand
Bottled prepared horseradish: on hand
Sugar: on hand
1 can (1 pound) Italian-style tomatoes with basil
1 small jar (about 5 ounces) pimiento-stuffed green olives
1 small tin (2 ounces) flat anchovy fillets
1 box (8½ ounces) thin chocolate wafers (about 36 wafers)
Confectioners' sugar: on hand
1 small bar (6 ounces) bittersweet chocolate
4 quarts club soda

FREEZER DEPARTMENT
1 pint vanilla ice cream
1 pint chocolate ice cream

HERBS, SPICES, AND SEASONINGS
Tabasco: on hand
Salt: on hand
Peppercorns
Paprika: on hand
Mixed Italian herbs
Dry mustard: on hand

PRODUCE DEPARTMENT

1 large green cabbage
6 tart crisp apples
2 bunches of parsley
Chives
1 head of Boston lettuce
Garlic: on hand
1 large purple onion: on hand
2 medium-sized tomatoes
6 oranges
6 lemons: have 3 on hand
3 limes

At the gourmet shop

1 box good-quality water biscuits
Escoffier Sauce Diable
Dijon-style mustard
Italian rice from Piedmont
Red-wine vinegar: on hand
Greek olives

At the delicatessen

1 pound top-quality liverwurst
½ pound hot Italian sausage
18 to 24 slices of rare roast beef

At the wine and liquor shop

Scotch
Vodka
Dry red wine: California jug wine
Light rum: on hand
Spanish brandy
Cognac

At the housewares shop

Paper napkins, large dark green
Paper book matches, dark green

At the ice company

Telephone for extra ice

Let someone else do the shopping while you take the morning off. For me there's a part-time helper, a college student who is majoring in home economics. When she arrives for work we discuss the menu and go over the list. She makes notes and is off and away while I go to have my hair done.

Any member of your family can, of course, do this job, but as anyone's free time is also valuable, a hired shopper can really be worth the small cost. Besides saving you, most shoppers can save money as well, especially if they are young high-school or college students; they love to shop, it's easy work, they usually need the money, and they will take a real interest in doing a professional job.

PREPARE PARTY FOOD IN ADVANCE

One week ahead prepare 2 ice-cream pies; serve one for tonight's dessert and store the other in the freezer for the party.

Several days ahead prepare 2 casseroles of the rice dish. Serve one as the main course for supper and store the other in the refrigerator for party fare.

Two nights before prepare double the amount of pâté. Serve some tonight; save the rest for the party.

One night ahead buy more roast beef than you need for the party. Serve the extra tonight.

◆

PÂTÉ LOUISE

1 pound top-quality liverwurst, room temperature
½ pound butter, at room temperature
2 to 3 tablespoons cognac or other good brandy
2 to 3 tablespoons Escoffier Sauce Diable
    or Worcestershire sauce
Coarse-ground black pepper
Salt
Paprika

Combine liverwurst with butter. First mash with a fork, then use a wooden spoon to beat and cream until smooth. Add cognac and Sauce Diable to taste. Season lightly with pepper and salt. Place in serving dish and sprinkle paprika over top.

MAKES 8 SERVINGS.

◆

Platter of
JELLIED SOUR-CREAM COLESLAW WITH SCANDINAVIAN BEET SALAD AND GREEN ASPARAGUS VINAIGRETTE

3 packages (3 ounces each) lemon-flavored gelatin
1 envelope unflavored gelatin
1 teaspoon salt
2 cups boiling water
2 cups cold water
4 tablespoons apple-cider vinegar
1 cup mayonnaise
2 cups sour cream
1 teaspoon prepared Dijon-style mustard
6 cups shredded cabbage
3 cups chopped unpeeled apple
1 can (1 pound) green asparagus, drained
Vinaigrette Dressing (recipe follows)
Lettuce
Parsley
Scandinavian Beet Salad (recipe follows)

Dissolve lemon-flavored gelatin, unflavored gelatin, and salt in the boiling water. Add cold water and vinegar. Stir in mayonnaise, sour cream, and mustard, blending thoroughly. Chill until thickened. Fold in cabbage and apple. Pour into 3 prepared 1½-quart molds. Chill until firm, about 3 hours. Marinate the drained asparagus in vinaigrette dressing; drain.

Unmold the jellied coleslaw onto a lettuce-lined long oval tray. Arrange asparagus and beet salad around the jellied coleslaw.

MAKES 20 SERVINGS.

VINAIGRETTE DRESSING

¼ *cup cider vinegar*

1 *tablespoon sugar*

½ *teaspoon salt*

¼ *teaspoon coarsely ground black pepper*

1 *cup safflower or peanut oil*

Place vinegar in a mixing bowl. Add sugar and beat with a fork or whisk until sugar has dissolved. Add salt and pepper. Slowly add oil, beating as it is added.

MAKES ABOUT 1⅓ CUPS DRESSING.

NOTE: If a more pungent flavor is desired, add ½ teaspoon dry mustard after adding sugar.

SCANDINAVIAN BEET SALAD

1 *can (1 pound) sliced beets*

½ *cup Vinaigrette Dressing (recipe above)*

½ *cup sour cream*

2 *tablespoons prepared horseradish*

1 *teaspoon sugar*

½ *teaspoon salt*

¼ *cup minced chives*

Drain beets; cut into julienne strips. Cover with vinaigrette dressing. Refrigerate for several hours.

Drain. Combine remaining ingredients and add to beets. Refrigerate until well chilled.

MAKES 6 SERVINGS IF SERVED AS A SEPARATE DISH, BUT WILL GARNISH LARGER AMOUNTS.

◆

RISO AL MODO DI GAUCHOS

½ pound hot Italian sausage
Water
2 tablespoons butter
2 tablespoons oil
1 garlic clove, peeled and minced
1 large purple onion, peeled and chopped
1 can (1 pound) Italian-style tomatoes with basil
1 teaspoon mixed Italian herbs
Salt
Pepper
5 cups cold cooked long-grain Carolina rice
    or Italian rice (see cooking instructions page 181)
1 small jar (about 5 ounces) pimiento-stuffed
    green olives, drained and coarsely chopped
¼ cup finely minced parsley

Place the sausage in a small skillet and cover with water. Bring to a boil, then reduce heat and let simmer for about 15 minutes. Pierce each sausage with the point of a small sharp knife to allow the fat to escape. Cook for about 5 additional minutes. Pierce them again with a knife, then drain. Set aside.

Combine butter and oil in a heavy skillet and place over moderate heat. When butter has melted, add the garlic and onion. Sauté until vegetables are limp, about 10 minutes. Add the tomatoes and bring to boiling. Stir in herbs and season to taste with salt and pepper. Reduce heat and let simmer until liquid has reduced to about half. Remove from heat. Let cool slightly.

Gently mix together sauce, cold rice, and chopped olives. Spoon into a well-buttered 2½- or 3-quart casserole dish. Slice the sausages and arrange them around the edge of the casserole. Can be made ahead to this point.

Bake casserole in preheated 350° F. oven for 20 to 30 minutes, or until all moisture has evaporated. Sprinkle with parsley and serve from the dish.

MAKES 8 OR MORE SERVINGS.

◆

COLD ROAST BEEF PLATTER

¼ cup red-wine vinegar
1 teaspoon salt
1 teaspoon dry mustard
¾ cup safflower oil
2 garlic cloves, peeled and split
18 to 24 slices of cold rare roast beef, about
    ¼ inch thick and trimmed of all fat
Freshly ground black pepper
Chopped parsley
Wedges of hard-cooked eggs, topped with anchovy strips
Greek ripe olives
Tomato wedges

To save time and effort, prepare this with delicatessen beef. Or if you prefer cook an eye round roast in advance, see Italian-Style Beef (recipe pages 162–63).

Combine vinegar, salt, and mustard and blend until smooth. Then slowly add oil, beating as it is added. Add garlic. Dip each slice of beef into this marinade and place it in a long shallow pan. Sprinkle each slice liberally with freshly ground black pepper and, with the back of a wooden spoon or the palm of your hand, press pepper into beef. Pour remaining marinade over meat. Cover and let stand at room temperature until ready to serve, or refrigerate until about 2 hours before serving, then bring to room temperature.

Drain the slices and arrange them slightly overlapping in the center of a large platter. Sprinkle with parsley. Surround with wedges of anchovy-topped hard-cooked eggs, olives, and tomato wedges.

MAKES 8 TO 12 SERVINGS.

◆

TIPSY ICE-CREAM PIE

4 tablespoons butter
1½ cups chocolate-wafer crumbs
¼ cup granulated sugar
1 pint vanilla ice cream
¼ cup cognac or good brandy
1 pint chocolate ice cream
¼ cup light rum
½ pint heavy cream
2 tablespoons confectioners' sugar
Grated bittersweet chocolate

Handwritten note at left: see Chot. for crust. P. 279 or Decon. whip.

Handwritten note at right: 3 c. Rice Krispies / ½ c. chopped nuts / 4 sq semi sweet / 2 T. butter or 6 oz choc chips. / Mix nuts + cereal / (crush some of cereal) / Melt choc + butter / stir into crumbs + nuts / Press in deep - greased / 10" pie plate

Preheat oven to 450° F.

In a large skillet melt the butter. Remove from heat and stir in crumbs and granulated sugar. Mix well. Press mixture against the bottom and sides of a 9-inch pie plate. Place in preheated oven and bake for 5 minutes. Cool crust, then refrigerate until chilled.

Let ice cream stand at room temperature to soften slightly. Do not allow to melt. Put a layer of vanilla ice cream in the bottom of the chilled crumb crust. Pour cognac over surface. Next add a layer of chocolate ice cream, mounding it high. Pour rum over surface. Place pie in freezer while whipping cream.

Whip cream until stiff. Fold in confectioners' sugar. Cover surface of pie with whipped cream. Using the large side of a hand grater, grate bittersweet chocolate over surface. Freeze pie until firm. Wrap in foil and seal. Store in freezer until about 20 minutes before cutting and serving.

To cut frozen pie easily, dip knife first into hot water.

MAKES 6 SERVINGS.

Come for
Drinks and
Stay for
a Casserole
Supper

◆

Casual, easy to prepare, and less elaborate than a cocktail buffet, this is the kind of get-together most everyone, both guests and party-giver, seems to prefer for weeknight after-work entertaining. It's a dinner, really, but the appetizers double as both first course and salad, while the casserole is the "meat-potatoes-vegetable." I usually add coffee but rarely a "made" dessert. Instead, I offer crisp little cookies from a good bakery or a small platter of fine imported chocolates.

Appetizers can be finger food and "make your own," or served from a tray. The casserole can be served from the pot or baking dish in which it was cooked. The only service necessary: plates, forks, and napkins. Everyone helps himself, and why not? You can even let everyone help you clean up.

Here are 3 menus to consider for this kind of party. Each menu is planned for 6 to 8 servings.

◆

CASSEROLE SUPPER #1

THE MENU

Garlicky Roasted Green-Pepper Strips
Brandied Black-Pepper Cheese

Red Wine

Lasagne
Party Rye Rounds   *Water Biscuits*

GARLICKY ROASTED GREEN-PEPPER STRIPS

3 large green peppers
2 garlic cloves, peeled and cut lengthwise into halves
3 tablespoons olive oil
2 teaspoons tarragon vinegar
Salt

Place peppers in the broiler about 3 inches from the heat source. Roast, turning often, until skins are flecked with black. Rinse under cold water and slip off skins. Cut into halves, remove seeds and all white membranes. Cut each half into about ½-inch strips.

Heat the garlic in the oil over moderate heat for 2 or 3 minutes. Remove from heat and add the vinegar. Pour over pepper strips in a long shallow nonmetal dish. Sprinkle lightly with salt. Turn strips until coated with dressing. Cover and refrigerate for several hours.

When ready to serve, drain and spear each strip with a cocktail pick. Serve cold.

MAKES 6 TO 8 SERVINGS.

◆

BRANDIED BLACK-PEPPER CHEESE

8 ounces cream cheese, at room temperature
2 or 3 tablespoons sour cream
2 tablespoons brandy
Coarse-ground black pepper, about ¼ cup
Water biscuits

Cream together cream cheese, sour cream, and brandy. Chill until firm enough to form into a log.

Roll cheese log in coarse-ground black pepper or grind pepper mill over surface. Press pepper firmly into cheese and refrigerate until ready to serve. Surround cheese with water biscuits and provide butter knife for spreading.

MAKES 8 SERVINGS.

◆

LASAGNE

An easy-to-make, budget, meatless version of this classic dish that is nonetheless hearty and filling. Easy-to-cook flat noodles are used instead of the traditional heavy lasagne noodles, and cottage cheese mixed with sour cream replaces the sometimes difficult-to-obtain ricotta cheese. Prepared ahead, it can be baked after your guests arrive, or can be baked ahead and reheated. It freezes well and can be reheated without thawing.

TOMATO SAUCE
3 *tablespoons butter*
1 *large purple onion, peeled and finely chopped*
1 *garlic clove, peeled and minced*
2 *large ripe tomatoes*
2 *cans (1 pound each) Italian-style tomatoes*
   with basil
3 *tablespoons tomato paste*
1 *cup water, more if needed*
1 *teaspoon mixed Italian herbs*
Salt
Pepper

Melt the butter in a large heavy pot. Add the onion and garlic and cook, stirring often, over low heat until soft. Slice the tomatoes into the pot and chop them with the tip of a spatula. Cook for about 5 minutes. Add remaining ingredients and stir to blend. Let sauce simmer, stirring often, for about 1 hour, or until thick. Adjust salt and pepper to taste. Set aside or refrigerate until ready to use. Reheat before preparing lasagne.

ASSEMBLING THE LASAGNE
1 pound flat noodles
Boiling water
Salt
1 tablespoon mild oil
2 tablespoons butter
1 pint creamy-style cottage cheese
1 cup sour cream
½ pound mozzarella cheese, cut into 1-inch dice
½ pound Parmesan cheese, grated
Tomato sauce

Cook noodles according to directions on pages 194–95, using your largest pot filled with boiling salted water to which you have added the oil. Drain noodles in a colander. Put butter in the still-warm cooking pot, add noodles, and fork-stir to coat with butter. Set aside.

In a mixing bowl combine cottage cheese and sour cream and blend with a fork. Stir in mozzarella cheese and three-fourths of the Parmesan.

In 2 baking dishes (each 12 x 8 x 2½ inches) place a thin layer of sauce. Cover with a layer of noodles. Add a layer of cheese mixture. Repeat twice with sauce, noodles, cheese. Cover final cheese layer with sauce and sprinkle remaining Parmesan cheese over surface. Bake lasagne, now or later, in a preheated 375° F. oven for 35 to 40 minutes. Let stand at room temperature for about 10 minutes before cutting and serving.

MAKES 8 TO 12 SERVINGS.

◆

CASSEROLE SUPPER #2

THE MENU

Artichoke Hearts Vinaigrette

Pâté Maison in Aspic
Toast Points

Island Chicken and Rice

Coffee with Anisette and Lemon Twists

◆

PÂTÉ MAISON IN ASPIC

ASPIC
2 *envelopes unflavored gelatin*
2 *cups chicken consommé*
2 *tablespoons Calvados or cognac or similar brandy*

PÂTÉ
1 *small tart apple, peeled, cored, and finely minced*
1 *small white onion, peeled and finely minced*
2 *tablespoons butter*
¼ *cup Calvados or cognac or similar brandy*
1 *pound liverwurst in one piece, at room temperature*
¼ *pound butter, at room temperature*
1 *teaspoon Worcestershire sauce*
Dash of Tabasco

Sprinkle gelatin over ½ cup of the consommé. Heat remaining consommé to boiling. Stir in softened gelatin and cold consommé. Stir until gelatin has dissolved. Add Calvados, cognac or brandy. Let stand to cool.

In a small skillet sauté minced apple and onion in the 2 tablespoons butter until very soft. When the apple is soft enough to mash with a spoon, transfer the whole mixture into the container of your electric blender and blend until smooth. Combine this with the liverwurst and butter in a large mixing bowl and with a wooden spoon cream all together until blended and smooth. Season with Worcestershire and Tabasco.

Pour sufficient cooled aspic mixture into a lightly oiled round, oblong, or melon mold to fill it to a depth of about 1 inch. Refrigerate until set. Spoon pâté mixture into center of mold over firm aspic. Cover top and sides with remaining cool liquid aspic mixture. Refrigerate until firm.

Unmold just before serving. Serve with Melba toast or unsalted crackers.

MAKES 8 SERVINGS.

◆

ISLAND CHICKEN AND RICE

2 frying chickens (each 2½ to 3 pounds)
    cut into serving pieces
Salt
1 tablespoon mild oil
1½ cups brown rice
2 tablespoons butter, at room temperature
1 cup coarsely chopped almonds
¾ cup raisins
2 to 3 tablespoons soy sauce

Place chicken pieces, not touching, in 1 or 2 long shallow pans. Place pans in cold oven and set temperature at 350° F. Let the chicken bake, turning frequently and basting with the rendered chicken fat, for about 1½ hours, or until each piece is fork tender. Chicken should be thoroughly cooked and the skin well browned and crisp. Remove from oven and pour off all fat. Sprinkle each piece with salt.

While chicken cooks, prepare rice. Fill a large kettle with about 2½ quarts water, add ½ teaspoon salt and the oil, and bring to a full boil. Slowly add rice. Reduce the heat and let rice boil gently for about 30 minutes, or until tender. Drain into a colander and pour boiling water over it to remove loose starch. Transfer dry hot rice to 1 or 2 long shallow casseroles. Stir in butter with a fork. When butter has melted add almonds and raisins. Fork-stir, then sprinkle generously with soy sauce; again fork-stir until each grain of rice is coated with soy sauce. Cover rice with baked chicken pieces. Cover baking dish (or dishes) with foil. Seal. Can be made ahead to this point.

Leave at room temperature for 1 to 2 hours. Then place in preheated 300° F. oven until heated. Or refrigerate until about 2 hours before serving, bring to room temperature, then reheat. Can be kept hot in 200° F. oven up to 1 hour.

MAKES 6 TO 8 SERVINGS.

◆

CASEROLE SUPPER #3

THE MENU

Cherry Tomatoes   Coarse Salt
Black Olives
Sliced Radishes   Sweet Butter
Thin-Sliced Black Bread
Sardines
Dijon-style Mustard
Thin-Sliced Sourdough Bread

Casserole of
Veal Marengo

Italian Chocolates
Italian-Irish Coffee

◆

VEAL MARENGO

12 *small white onions*
¼ *pound salt pork, cut into small cubes*
3 *pounds lean shoulder of veal, cubed*
2 *tablespoons butter*
2 *medium-sized onions, peeled and finely chopped*
½ *garlic clove, peeled and finely minced*
1 *tablespoon flour*
2 *cups chicken stock or broth*
1 *cup dry white wine*
½ *cup tomato purée*
1 *bay leaf*
Dash of Tabasco
½ *teaspoon Worcestershire sauce*
Salt
Pepper
3 *tomatoes*
1 *can (4 ounces) mushroom slices sautéed in butter*

Peel the onions. Place in a saucepan and cover with water. Bring to a full boil, then let simmer for about 5 minutes. Drain. Cover with fresh water and let simmer until tender. Drain and set aside.

Cover pork cubes with water in a saucepan. Bring to a full boil and then let simmer for about 5 minutes. Drain and pat dry. Place the blanched pork cubes in a large ceramic-coated cast-iron or similar heavy pot and let cook over low heat until all fat has been rendered and cubes are crisp. Remove cubes with a slotted spoon to paper toweling to drain. Set aside. Pour all but a thin film of fat from the pot into a small bowl or pitcher. Set aside.

Heat the fat remaining in the pot to almost sizzling. Add 6 or 8 veal cubes and cook, turning them with a wooden spoon, until lightly browned. Remove them to a large bowl or platter. Add a little of the reserved rendered fat and continue browning the meat, a few pieces at a time, until all are browned, adding rendered fat as needed.

Pour any remaining fat from pot and add butter. When melted add the chopped onions and minced garlic. Cook, stirring, over low heat until limp. Stir in the flour, then slowly add the stock, stirring as it is added. Add the wine and stir in the tomato purée. Return the browned meat to the pot. Stir to distribute evenly, then add bay leaf, Tabasco, and Worcestershire. Season to taste with salt and pepper. Cover and let simmer for about 1 hour, or until meat is tender. Add additional stock or wine if needed.

Cut tomatoes into wedges and squeeze out seeds. Add tomato wedges, boiled onions, and mushrooms to veal mixture and continue cooking for about 10 minutes, or until vegetables are hot.

MAKES 6 TO 8 SERVINGS.

◆

ITALIAN-IRISH COFFEE

1 ounce coffee liqueur
Hot, just-made, strong black coffee
2 tablespoons heavy cream, whipped almost stiff
*   and flavored with 1 teaspoon white Crème*
*   de Menthe*
Shaved bittersweet chocolate

Pour liqueur into an Irish coffee glass or any heavy stemmed glass that holds 8 ounces. Put a silver spoon in the glass to keep it from cracking when you add the hot coffee. Pour in sufficient coffee to come to about 2 inches of rim. Top with the flavored whipped cream and sprinkle with shaved chocolate.

MAKES 1 DRINK.

Open-House
Cocktail
Buffet

Even if your guest list is long, an open-house cocktail-buffet party is easy to put together, needn't cost a bundle, and can be marvelous fun.

It's especially great for winter holiday and vacation-time entertaining (Christmas week or New Year's Eve) when many other parties are also being given. You can ask every one of your friends, safe in the knowledge that though almost all will accept, many will not be free for the entire evening, which means you can go all out in the hospitality department without overcrowding your house or apartment and without totally wrecking your budget. People come and go as they like, stay for several hours, or just drop by for one drink. So no matter how many you invite altogether, there's no need to prepare large quantities of any one dish.

Instead you can offer a sufficient variety of hot and cold food to suit the different appetites of your guests—those who come early for "cocktails and hors d'oeuvres" before going elsewhere for dinner, those who come for the evening and expect what you serve to *be* dinner, and those who have had dinner before coming to your house for coffee, dessert, and liqueurs.

I think of the menu for this type of party in several parts. Invite everyone for from 6:30 on, whenever they can make the scene, early or late, then prepare for each part.

Part I: From 6:30 to about 7:45, serve drinks plus a variety of hot and cold appetizers, as many or as few as time-to-prepare and money will allow.

Part II: About 8 o'clock set out a buffet supper, 2 or more hot casseroles (1 meatless, 1 made with meat, chicken, or seafood), a cold meat platter, 1 or several salads, plus good breads, condiments and such. With the buffet I usually have wine available.

Part III: Around 10 o'clock offer a choice of coffee, dessert, and liqueurs, or an after-dinner drink.

If this all sounds like a lot of work, remember that almost all the food can be prepared in easy stages 1 or 2 days before the party. Service can be as casual as you care to make it and can be easily coped with, as not all guests will come at the same time.

◆

PART I:
APPETIZERS, HOT AND COLD,
TO SERVE WITH DRINKS

Select as many appetizers, some hot and some cold, as your equipment and space will allow. Prepare enough of any one to make 6 to 12 appetizer servings. For 50 guests you might choose 6 appetizers and prepare enough of each to make 12 servings, or, if you have enough serving dishes and space to present them, choose 12 appetizers and prepare enough of each to make 6 servings. Appetites vary, and sometimes you will have guests who eat very little. Those friends who plan to stay for buffet supper probably won't eat huge amounts at this stage because they will be anticipating the main-course dishes that will be served later in the evening.

◆

CURTAIN RAISERS

Spear pitted black or green olives with crisp carrot sticks.

Brush thin slices of raw turnip with lemon juice. Spread with soft Cheddar cheese.

Use sardines that are packed in mustard sauce. Mash them, season with Worcestershire, Tabasco, black pepper, and salt. Stuff large raw mushroom caps with mixture.

Dip cold cooked asparagus into mayonnaise. Wrap in paper-thin slices of prosciutto or baked Virginia ham. Secure with cocktail picks.

Cut small peeled cucumbers into strips. Wrap each strip in a thin slice of smoked salmon and secure with cocktail picks.

Scoop out the centers of small cooked and chilled Brussels sprouts, then fill with equal parts of blue cheese and cream cheese thinned with a little cognac or other good brandy.

Spread thin slices of dried beef with cream cheese. Cover with chopped watercress and chives. Roll up and secure with cocktail picks.

Scoop out the centers of small boiled (canned or home-cooked) chilled white onions. Fill with Smithfield ham spread. Press a small pimiento-stuffed olive into the center.

Marinate thin strips of raw zucchini in French dressing. Drain. Wrap an anchovy fillet around each strip and secure with cocktail picks.

Wash a pint of fresh Bing cherries. Place in a nonmetal bowl and add 1 cup of dry white wine. Refrigerate for 6 hours or longer. Drain just before serving.

Peel a large fresh pineapple and cut into bite-sized wedges. Place in a nonmetal bowl and add 1 cup of gin and 2 tablespoons chopped chives. Toss to blend. Refrigerate for 6 hours or longer. Drain just before serving.

Brush slices of crisp tart apples with lemon juice. Cream equal parts of Roquefort cheese and cream cheese with sufficient cognac to make a smooth spread. Cover apple slices with mixture mounded high and sprinkle with chives.

Wrap peeled whole figs in paper-thin slices of prosciutto and secure with cocktail picks.

Marinate fresh pineapple chunks in Jamaica rum for 6 hours or overnight. Drain. Wrap each cube in a strip of bacon. Broil until bacon is crisp.

Peel ripe but firm peaches and cut into bite-sized chunks. Marinate in French dressing (made with 3 parts oil to 1 part fresh lemon juice) for 2 to 3 hours. Drain. Sprinkle with chives and spear each cube with a cocktail pick.

Marinate small clusters of grapes in Marsala wine for 12 to 24 hours. Drain and serve with wedges of Switzerland Swiss cheese.

◆

WORCESTERSHIRE CHEESE

8 ounces cream cheese
Worcestershire sauce
Seasoned salt
Unsalted crackers

Place cream cheese on serving plate. Pour Worcestershire sauce over entire surface; be generous. Sprinkle with seasoned salt. Surround with crackers. Stick 2 small butter knives into cheese.
MAKES 8 SERVINGS.

◆

ANCHOVY CHEESE

8 ounces cream cheese
1 can (2 ounces) rolled anchovies stuffed
    with capers, packed in oil
Unsalted crackers

Place cream cheese on serving plate. Dump anchovies and oil from can over surface. Surround with crackers. Stick 2 small butter knives into center of cheese.
MAKES 8 SERVINGS.

◆

SAUSAGE BALLS

½ pound spicy-hot country pork sausage meat
Dijon-style mustard, in stoneware crock

Roll sausage into 1-inch balls, or smaller. Place in a large skillet. Cover with water and let simmer for about 5 minutes. Drain off water. Fry, turning often, until lightly browned and no longer pink in the center. Spear each sausage ball with a cocktail pick.

Place the crock of mustard in center of a round serving plate. Arrange sausage balls around crock.

MAKES 6 SERVINGS.

◆

CHAFING-DISH DEVILED OYSTERS

1 *pint large oysters*
2 *tablespoons butter, at room temperature*
2 *tablespoons Worcestershire sauce*
2 *tablespoons prepared horseradish*
1 *tablespoon lemon juice*
Packaged cocktail puffs

Drain oysters and place in a chafing dish or electric skillet with butter and Worcestershire sauce. Cook over low heat until edges curl. Stir in horseradish and lemon juice. Have cocktail picks nearby. Let guests spear their own oysters onto cocktail puffs.

MAKES 6 SERVINGS.

NOTE: This is what I call a "show-off" dish that is prepared after guests have arrived. Just arrange all ingredients on a tray and carry to wherever you have set up your chafing dish or electric skillet.

◆

HOT CHEESE PUFFS

1 *pound firm white bread* (*20 slices, or more*)
1 *cup firm real mayonnaise*
½ *to ¾ pound Parmesan cheese, grated*
½ *large purple onion, peeled*

Cut crusts from bread (save for bread crumbs). Cut each slice into 3 strips. Toast on one side. This much can be done ahead.

Combine mayonnaise with grated cheese in a small mixing bowl. Place a flat hand grater over the bowl and grate onion directly into mixture. (Save the last bit of onion, wrapped in plastic wrap, for later use.)

Spread can be made ahead and bread strips toasted, but it is best to assemble them just before broiling.

Preheat broiler. Spread untoasted side of bread strips with mayonnaise mixture and place in broiler 3 or 4 inches from heat source until well puffed, about 5 minutes. Serve hot.

MAKES 12 OR MORE SERVINGS.

◆

PUFF PASTE PIZZAS

12 frozen patty shells
½ pound small pepperoni, very thinly sliced
½ cup grated Parmesan cheese
2 tablespoons crushed dried oregano
1 can (10 ounces) pizza sauce
6 ounces mozzarella cheese, very thinly sliced
*   and torn into pieces*

Remove frozen patty shells from packages and let thaw at room temperature until soft but still cold.

Roll out patty shells, 2 or 3 at a time, on a lightly floured board. With a small cooky cutter, cut 2 rounds from each circle of dough. Turn up edges of each round slightly to form a rim. Place rounds, not touching, on 2 long baking sheets. Place baking sheets in freezer until dough has refrozen and is very firm.

When ready to bake and serve, preheat oven to 400° F.

Remove baking sheets from freezer and cover each little round with 2 or 3 slices of pepperoni. Sprinkle with Parmesan cheese and oregano. Add about 1 tablespoon of sauce and cover with a small piece of mozzarella. Sprinkle a little more Parmesan over surface. Bake in preheated oven for about 10 minutes, or until rim of crust is lightly browned and cheese has melted. Serve hot.

MAKES 24 MINIATURE PIZZAS.

◆

QUICHE ITALIENNE

4 eggs
1 tablespoon tomato paste
1 cup cream
Dash of Tabasco
Dash of seasoned salt
¼ cup grated Parmesan cheese
⅓ cup shredded prosciutto
1 frozen pie shell, 9 inches

Preheat oven to 400° F.

In a mixing bowl beat eggs with tomato paste until thoroughly blended. Add cream, Tabasco, seasoned salt, and Parmesan cheese. Blend well. Sprinkle shredded prosciutto over bottom of frozen pie shell. Pour in egg mixture. Place pie on a baking sheet. Bake for 10 minutes at 400° F. Reduce oven to 350° F. and continue to bake until custard is firm, about 20 minutes.

Cut into wedges and serve hot or warm. Quiche can be kept at room temperature and will stay warm enough to serve for about 1 hour.

Can be made ahead. Cover and refrigerate until time to reheat. Let stand at room temperature for about 1 hour. Reheat in 350° F. oven for about 10 minutes.

MAKES 6 TO 8 SERVINGS.

◆

CHINESE ROAST PORK STRIPS

⅓ cup soy sauce
3 tablespoons hoisin sauce*
2 garlic cloves, peeled and minced
⅓ cup honey
½ teaspoon five-spice powder** (optional)
½ cup boiling water
8-rib loin of pork, boned and cut lengthwise
    into halves, making 2 long strips

ACCOMPANIMENTS
Plum sauce
Chinese mustard

Combine first 5 ingredients. Add boiling water and stir until honey is dissolved. Place pork in a shallow glass pan and pour marinade over it. Cover and refrigerate for several hours, turning the meat occasionally.

Wipe meat dry; place on a rack in a shallow pan. Roast, uncovered, at 300° F. for 1½ hours, spooning marinade over it frequently. Allow meat to stand at room temperature for 1 hour before carving.

Cut room-temperature meat into thin slices. Cut slices into strips. Serve with Chinese mustard and plum sauce as dips. Serve at room temperature.

MAKES 12 SERVINGS.

*HOISIN SAUCE
You'll find *hoisin* sauce, in cans, at almost any Oriental grocery store and in many large supermarkets. Sweet and spicy, it's made of soybeans, sugar, garlic, and salt but tastes vaguely like a rich preserve. You've probably eaten it in a Chinese restaurant where chefs use it both in cooking and as an accompaniment to roast pork, Peking duck, and such. It isn't very expensive, and it's

well worth the trouble. Serve it with any pork dish, with roast chicken, with duck, etc.

**FIVE-SPICE POWDER

Like curry powder, this is a blend of spices used by Oriental cooks for seasoning many dishes. The spices are star anise, licorice root, cinnamon, fennel, and cloves. Use for roast pork, spareribs, chicken, or duck. You'll find it at Oriental markets and at some large supermarkets.

◆

OYSTER RAMEKINS

8 to 10 green onions
½ pound butter
1 garlic clove, peeled and split lengthwise
¼ teaspoon salt
Pinch of thyme
2 tablespoons cognac or other good brandy
Fine dry bread crumbs, about 1 cup
½ cup chopped shallots
2 dozen large raw oysters
2 tablespoons dry white wine

Finely mince the green onions. Melt ¼ pound of the butter with the garlic in a small skillet over low heat. Bring to almost sizzling. Remove from heat and let cool to room temperature. Remove and discard garlic. Add salt, thyme, and cognac or brandy. Blend in sufficient bread crumbs to form mixture into a log. Place log on a sheet of foil or a flat baking sheet in freezer until very firm. Wrap in foil or plastic wrap and store in freezer or refrigerator. When ready to use, let log stand at room temperature until it can be easily sliced.

Sauté shallots in remaining ¼ pound butter until limp. Add oysters and wine. Let simmer until edges of oysters curl. Divide oysters, shallots, and a little of the cooking liquid equally among 6 to 8 individual ramekins and top each with a slice of butter mixture. Can be made ahead to this point. Cover ramekins and refrigerate until ready to bake.

Preheat oven to 375° F.

Place ramekins on a baking sheet in preheated oven for 8 to 10 minutes, or until sizzling hot.

To serve, place hot ramekins on small plates. Provide cocktail forks.

MAKES 6 TO 8 SERVINGS.

◆

CHICKEN LIVERS AND MUSHROOMS IN VERMOUTH

1 pound large fresh mushrooms
½ pound butter
2 tablespoons lemon juice
2 pounds chicken livers
Ice water
Salt
Pepper
Flour
3 garlic cloves, peeled
1 cup sweet vermouth
48 prepared packaged tart shells, about 2-inch size

Trim mushrooms and slice diagonally. Sauté in 4 tablespoons of the butter over moderate heat for about 10 minutes. Add lemon juice. Cook for an additional 2 or 3 minutes. Set aside.

Wash and trim chicken livers. Cover with ice water and let stand for 30 minutes. Drain and pat dry with paper toweling. Cut each liver into halves. Sprinkle with salt and pepper, and dust lightly with flour.

Melt about half of the remaining butter with the garlic in a large heavy skillet. Add half of the chicken livers and cook over high heat, shaking the pan so that they do not stick. Cook until lightly browned. Remove from pan with slotted spatula and set aside. Add remaining butter to skillet. When melted add remaining livers and sauté in the same manner.

Return the first batch of cooked livers to the pan and add the mushrooms and their butter. Remove and discard garlic. Add the vermouth. Let cook until vermouth is reduced to about half. Can be made ahead to this point.

When ready to serve, transfer mixture to chafing dish or electric skillet. Provide a serving spoon and a tray of small prepared tart shells. Let guests fill their own.

MAKES ABOUT 24 SERVINGS.

NOTE: If livers and mushrooms become too dry, simply add a little slightly heated vermouth.

◆

SESAME SHRIMPS

1 pound jumbo raw shrimps (about 16)
¼ cup soy sauce
¼ cup dry sherry
1 cup vegetable oil
½ teaspoon sesame-seed oil

Peel and devein shrimps. Combine remaining ingredients and pour over shrimps in a nonmetal bowl. Cover and refrigerate for 8 to 12 hours.

When ready to serve, place in a shallow pan with the oil that clings to them and broil, turning once with a spatula, for 6 to 8 minutes. Don't overcook or they will become tough.

MAKES ABOUT 8 SERVINGS.

◆

PICKLED BEETS WITH SOUR CREAM

1 can (1 pound) whole baby beets (about 12)
½ cup sugar
1½ cups white-wine vinegar
2 bay leaves
1 small onion, peeled and sliced
1 small piece of fresh horseradish
1 cup sour cream mixed with 1 tablespoon
  chopped chives

Drain beets. Combine sugar, vinegar, and bay leaves. Place over medium heat and stir until sugar dissolves. Add beets. Bring to a boil and boil for 1 minute. Cool. Add onion and horseradish. Transfer to a nonmetal refrigerator storage dish. Cover and refrigerate until time to serve. Drain. Spear each beet with a cocktail pick.

Place a bowl of sour cream in the center of a round serving plate. Arrange beets around dip. Serve while cold.

MAKES 6 SERVINGS.

◆

FLAGEOLETS VINAIGRETTE

2 jars or cans (1 pound each) flageolets
  (imported pale green beans)
1 cup salad oil
¼ cup white-wine vinegar
1 garlic clove, peeled and cut into halves
1 large white onion, peeled and finely chopped
½ cup chopped ripe olives
½ teaspoon salt
¼ teaspoon freshly ground black pepper
½ cup finely chopped parsley

Drain beans and combine with remaining ingredients. Cover and refrigerate for 4 to 12 hours.

Remove garlic. Drain off excess liquid. Provide small cocktail forks and serve on small plates.

MAKES 6 TO 8 SERVINGS.

◆

ARTICHOKE HEARTS WITH ANCHOVY FILLETS

¼ cup olive oil
1 garlic clove, peeled and cut into halves
2 packages (9 ounces each) frozen artichoke hearts
1 small jar (4½ ounces) button mushrooms, drained
2 tablespoons fresh lemon juice
6 anchovy fillets, drained and chopped
Freshly ground black pepper
Salt

Heat the oil with the garlic in a large skillet. Add the frozen artichoke hearts and cook over low heat until defrosted and hot. Remove garlic and stir in mushrooms. Transfer to a nonmetal bowl and add lemon juice and anchovy fillets. Toss lightly and season generously with pepper. Taste and add salt if desired. Cover and refrigerate until chilled.

Drain off excess liquid. Serve on small plates and provide cocktail forks.

MAKES 6 TO 8 SERVINGS.

◆

BRANDIED MUSHROOMS AND BLACK OLIVES

1 pound small button mushrooms
3 tablespoons oil
1 tablespoon lemon juice
1 garlic clove, peeled
Salt
Freshly ground black pepper
1 small can (6 ounces) pitted black olives, drained
¼ cup cognac or other good brandy

Place mushrooms, oil, lemon juice, and garlic in a small saucepan and cook, stirring often, over moderate heat for 8 to 10 minutes. Pour into a nonmetal bowl and sprinkle lightly with salt and pepper. Add olives and cognac. Refrigerate for 6 hours or longer.

Drain and serve with cocktail picks for spearing.

MAKES 6 TO 8 SERVINGS.

◆

VEGETABLE HORS D'OEUVRE VARIÉS

6 to 8 small young carrots, scraped and
    cut into finger-length sticks
1 small cauliflower, cut into flowerets
6 to 8 canned tiny white onions
1 small jar (6 ounces) artichoke hearts, drained
6 to 8 canned very small whole baby beets
¾ cup salad oil
¼ cup white-wine vinegar
1 tablespoon salt
½ tablespoon freshly ground black pepper
½ teaspoon sugar
1 garlic clove, peeled (optional)
8 to 10 large black olives
6 to 8 cherry tomatoes
Mustard Mayonnaise (recipe follows)
Hot Anchovy Dip (recipe follows)

Cook carrots and cauliflower in boiling salted water until just
barely tender. Drain. While still warm combine with other
vegetables in a large nonmetal bowl. Add oil, vinegar, salt,
pepper, sugar, and garlic. Cover and let marinate in the refrigerator until well chilled.

Remove garlic. Add olives and tomatoes. Toss well. Drain
off marinade and arrange vegetables on a large serving platter.
Serve with cocktail picks and fondue forks for easy dunking into
choice of cold Mustard Mayonnaise or Hot Anchovy Dip.

MAKES 6 TO 8 SERVINGS.

MUSTARD MAYONNAISE

1 cup mayonnaise
1 tablespoon lemon juice
2 tablespoons prepared Dijon-style or
Dusseldorf-style mustard
½ cup sour cream
Salt
Freshly ground black pepper
Paprika

Combine mayonnaise, lemon juice, and mustard. Beat with a wire whisk until blended. Fold in sour cream. Add salt and pepper to taste. Chill. Dust with paprika just before serving.

MAKES 1½ CUPS.

HOT ANCHOVY DIP

¼ pound butter
¾ cup olive oil
1 garlic clove, peeled and mashed
8 to 10 anchovy fillets, chopped
½ cup finely minced parsley
Freshly ground black pepper
Salt

Combine butter and oil in a fondue pot or chafing dish over medium heat. Add garlic and anchovy fillets. Heat to steaming. Add parsley. Season generously with pepper. Taste and add salt if desired. Keep warm over low heat.

Let guests dunk prepared vegetables into dip before eating "hot from the pot."

MAKES 1½ CUPS.

◆

PART II:
BUFFET SUPPER FOR COCKTAIL BUFFET

CASSEROLE DISHES

◆

CANNELLINI CASSEROLE

2 cans (1 pound each) cannellini or other white beans
1 garlic clove, peeled and minced
1 small purple onion, peeled and finely chopped
2 tablespoons olive oil
1 can (1 pound) Italian-style tomatoes with basil
1 teaspoon tomato paste
1 large ripe but firm tomato, peeled, seeded,
    and chopped
1 teaspoon mixed Italian herbs
½ teaspoon salt, more as needed
Freshly ground black pepper
2 tablespoons tarragon vinegar
½ cup finely minced parsley

Drain the *cannellini* into a colander and rinse under cold water until water runs through clear. Drain and blot dry with paper toweling. Sauté the garlic and onion in the olive oil in a large oven-to-table casserole. When vegetables are limp add the beans, canned tomatoes, tomato paste, fresh tomato, herbs, and salt. Mix together gently but thoroughly. Bring to boiling point on top of the stove, then cover and place in a preheated 375° F. oven for 20 to 30 minutes. Can be made ahead to this point. Refrigerate. Bring to room temperature, then reheat in oven or on top of stove over moderate heat.

Just before serving, stir in vinegar and taste for seasoning.

Add additional salt and freshly ground pepper as needed; gently stir in parsley. Keep hot on a warming tray on the buffet.

MAKES 8 TO 10 SERVINGS.

◆

CHILI MACARONI CASSEROLE

2 tablespoons butter
½ pound top round of beef, ground
½ cup chopped onion
1 tablespoon chili powder
2 cans (1 pound each) chile con carne with beans
1 pound elbow macaroni, cooked and drained
1 cup chopped parsley
1 cup shredded Jack or any semifirm mild cheese

Melt butter in a heavy skillet. Add beef and cook, stirring occasionally, until beef is no longer pink. Add onion, cover, and cook for about 5 minutes. Stir in chili powder. Add chile con carne and stir until heated. Remove from heat. Mix in drained macaroni, parsley, and cheese. Transfer to 2 long, shallow baking dishes. Bake in a 350° F. oven until cheese is melted, about 25 minutes.

MAKES 8 TO 10 SERVINGS.

◆

TEXAS SAUSAGE BEAN CASSEROLE

1 pound well-seasoned country-style sausage
2 tablespoons butter
1 cup chopped onions
4 cans (1 pound each) baked beans in tomato sauce
2 tablespoons apple-cider vinegar
¼ cup hot mustard
½ cup dark brown sugar

In a heavy skillet fry sausage until browned. Drain off fat. Melt butter in another skillet over low heat. Add onions and cook, stirring frequently, for 8 to 10 minutes, or until very soft. Add sausage and onions to beans in a large deep baking dish. Stir in vinegar and mustard. Add brown sugar and mix gently until blended. Cover and bake at 325° F. for 1 hour. Simple but good.

MAKES 8 TO 12 SERVINGS.

◆

DEVILED OYSTER CASSEROLE

1½ quarts oysters, drained
2 cups bread crumbs made from day-old French bread
4 eggs, beaten
2 cups light cream
1 teaspoon salt
1 cup Escoffier Sauce Diable
1 teaspoon Worcestershire sauce
2 to 3 dashes of Tabasco
¼ cup chopped parsley

Combine all ingredients and pour into a well-buttered 3-quart casserole. Can be prepared several hours ahead. Cover casserole with foil and refrigerate until time to bake. Bake at 350° F. for 35 to 40 minutes.

Recipe can be doubled, but in that case it should be baked in 2 casseroles rather than in 1 larger one.

MAKES 8 TO 10 SERVINGS.

◆

SHRIMP CASSEROLE

3 *pounds raw shrimps*
2 *cans (10 ounces each) condensed cream of*
    mushroom soup
1½ *cups commercial sour cream*
¼ *cup cognac or other good brandy*
3 *tablespoons butter*
1 *small white onion, peeled and minced*
1 *tablespoon curry powder*
Paprika
Toast points

Fill a large pot with water and bring to a full boil. Add shrimps and let boil until shells turn pink. Stir with a long-handled spoon to distribute shrimps in boiling water. Don't overcook; 2 or 3 minutes should be sufficient. Drain, shell, and devein.

Combine shrimps, soup, sour cream, and cognac in a large mixing bowl. Melt butter in a small saucepan. Add onion and sauté until limp. Stir in curry powder and cook, stirring, for a few seconds. Add to shrimp mixture and stir to blend. Cover bowl and refrigerate for several hours to allow flavors to mellow and blend.

Preheat oven to 325° F.

Transfer mixture to a long shallow baking dish and bake only until heated, about 30 minutes. Sprinkle with paprika. Serve over toast points.

MAKES 12 SERVINGS, OR MORE.

◆

COLD ROAST PORK
WITH MELON AND OLIVES

4½ to 5 pounds pork loin roast
3 garlic cloves
1 teaspoon crushed dried rosemary
1 teaspoon dried thyme
3 teaspoons salt
1 teaspoon coarse-ground black pepper
1 large yellow onion, peeled and thinly sliced
1 cup dry white wine, more if needed
1 cup orange juice
1 large or 2 small honeydew melons
Juice from 1 lemon
Ripe olives (preferably Greek or Italian)
Lemon wedges
Parsley sprigs

Wipe meat dry. Peel the garlic and cut into slivers. With a small sharp knife force garlic slivers deep into meat on both sides. Combine herbs, salt, and pepper. Rub mixture into meat. Wrap meat tightly in foil and refrigerate for 12 to 24 hours.

Unwrap meat and let stand at room temperature for about 1 hour before roasting.

Preheat oven to 475° F.

Arrange sliced onion on the bottom of a roasting pan and place the roast on top. Pour wine over surface. Bake uncovered for 15 to 20 minutes, or until meat is golden brown. Reduce heat to 325° F. and continue to roast for a total of 30 minutes to the pound. Baste often, using more wine if necessary. After about 2 hours of roasting, pour orange juice over meat and cover roast lightly with foil. Continue to roast until done.

Cool and slice. Arrange slices in a long shallow pan; cover tightly with foil. Refrigerate. Pour pan juice into a shallow bowl and place in freezer until fat congeals on surface. Remove fat and pour juices over meat. Cover and refrigerate until about 30 minutes before time to serve. Drain the meat and arrange slices on a serving platter. Peel and seed melon and cut into thin wedges. Sprinkle with lemon juice. Arrange alternate slices of roast and melon wedges on serving platter. Scatter olives over both meat and melon. Garnish with lemon wedges and parsley sprigs.

MAKES 8 TO 10 SERVINGS.

◆

BRAISED VEAL WITH PICKLED PEACHES AND CRANBERRY-HORSERADISH RELISH

2 tablespoons vegetable oil
1 neck of veal, boned and tied—about 4½ to 5 pounds
    after it has been boned
3 tablespoons butter
1 garlic clove, peeled and minced
2 medium-sized onions, peeled and chopped
½ cup chopped mushroom stems
1 cup dry white wine
Salt
Pepper
Pickled Peaches, canned
Cranberry-Horseradish relish (recipe follows)
Watercress

Preheat oven to 350° F.

Heat the oil in a heavy skillet until it smokes. Add the veal and brown it lightly on all sides. In a flame-proof casserole with a tight-fitting cover, just large enough to hold the meat rather snugly, melt the butter. Add the garlic, onions, and mushrooms and cook, stirring often, for about 10 minutes.

Place the meat on top of the vegetables and pour in the wine. Sprinkle liberally with salt and pepper. Cover and bring to a full boil over high heat, then transfer the casserole to the preheated oven. Bake for 1½ hours, or until the veal is tender. Baste after 30 minutes, then continue basting every 15 minutes. The meat is done when the juices run golden rather than pink when pierced with a small sharp knife.

Transfer the veal to a platter and let stand for 25 to 30 minutes. Cut away string. The veal may, of course, be served warm, but for buffet purposes, refrigerate covered. Strain the braising sauce into a nonmetal bowl and refrigerate until all the fat rises to the surface and congeals. Remove and discard fat. Reheat juices to boiling.

Cut the cold veal into thin slices and place the slices slightly overlapping in a long shallow nonmetal pan. Pour the hot strained juices over them. Cover the pan with foil and store in the refrigerator until time to serve.

Drain veal slices and arrange on a large round platter alternately with pickled peaches and mounds of cranberry-horseradish relish. Garnish with sprigs of watercress.

MAKES ABOUT 10 SERVINGS.

NOTE: Any solid piece of veal can be braised as desired. The neck, however, is one of the least expensive cuts, and though you will find a bit of cartilage occasionally (your butcher will have removed most of the cartilage when it is being boned) the flavor is excellent, and it is easy to carve into uniform slices. The neck must be ordered in advance as it is usually cut into chunks or ground for veal patties.

CRANBERRY-HORSERADISH RELISH

2 cups fresh or frozen cranberries
½ cup water
1 cup sugar
½ cup prepared horseradish

Combine cranberries and water in a saucepan. Cover and bring to a boil over medium heat. Let simmer until skins burst. Remove from heat. Stir in sugar and horseradish. Mix well. Cool, then refrigerate until well chilled.

MAKES ABOUT 2 CUPS.

◆

BRAISED HAM WITH WALDORF SALAD, PARSLEY, AND GRAPES

4 to 5 pounds fully cooked, mildly smoked half ham
4 cups unsweetened canned pineapple juice
½ cup apple-cider vinegar
4 to 6 red hot peppers, chopped (optional)
½ cup light brown sugar
1 tablespoon dry mustard
½ teaspoon ground cloves
Waldorf Salad (recipe follows)
Parsley sprigs
Purple grapes

Have your butcher remove the rind and all but a very thin layer of fat from the ham. Place it fat side up in a heavy pot, one large enough to leave some space between the top of the ham and the lid.

Combine next 6 ingredients in a saucepan. Cook, stirring, over medium heat until the sugar has dissolved. Bring to a boil and pour boiling over ham. Cover the pot and let simmer over low heat for about 1 hour; baste frequently. Turn the ham fat side down for the last 15 minutes of cooking.

Transfer the ham to a carving board and let cool. Using a sharp knife, cut meat into thin slices. Place slices slightly overlapping in 2 long shallow baking dishes. Cover and refrigerate. Refrigerate braising liquid until it is cold and all fat has risen to the surface and congealed. Remove and discard fat. Place liquid over medium heat and let simmer until reduced to about

2 cups. Cool slightly, then pour over ham slices. Refrigerate until ready to serve.

To serve, bring to room temperature, then drain slices and arrange around a mound of Waldorf salad on a large round serving platter. Garnish with parsley and small clusters of purple grapes.

MAKES 8 SERVINGS.

WALDORF SALAD

3 cups diced apples
1 cup diced celery
1 cup broken walnuts
1 cup halved green seedless grapes
¼ cup mayonnaise
½ teaspoon lemon juice
½ cup sour cream
Salt

Combine diced apples, celery, walnuts, and grapes. Blend together mayonnaise, lemon juice, and sour cream. Fold into apple mixture. Season to taste with salt.

MAKES 8 TO 12 BUFFET SERVINGS.

◆

ITALIAN-STYLE BEEF WITH HOT MUSTARD

½ teaspoon garlic salt
1 tablespoon mixed Italian herbs
1 teaspoon coarse-ground black pepper
½ teaspoon salt
4½ to 5 pounds eye of beef round
2 strips of bacon
Hot mustard
Radish roses
Cucumber slices
Small sour pickles

Mix seasonings together and rub into entire surface of meat. Wrap tightly in aluminum foil. Refrigerate for 12 to 24 hours.

When ready to proceed, unwrap meat and bring to room temperature.

Preheat oven to 325° F.

Blanch bacon slices; cover with boiling water in a small saucepan and boil for 1 minute. Drain and pat thoroughly dry with paper toweling. Fry blanched bacon in a large heavy skillet over moderate heat until crisp. Remove bacon (reserve for another use). Pour off all but about 1 tablespoon of the rendered bacon fat. Heat to almost smoking. Add beef and brown on all sides.

Transfer browned meat to a roasting pan and place in preheated oven. Roast for 18 minutes to the pound for rare, 20 to 22 minutes to the pound for medium-rare.

Bring meat to room temperature and slice. Place a small bowl of hot mustard in the center of a large round platter. Arrange meat around the bowl of mustard. Garnish platter with radish roses, cucumber slices, and small sour pickles.

MAKES 10 TO 12 SERVINGS.

◆

CORN AND RICE SALAD
WITH SHRIMPS AND MAYONNAISE ROUGE

1 cup fresh corn kernels, cut from 2 or 3
    ears of corn, or substitute thoroughly defrosted
    frozen corn kernels
1 tablespoon cider vinegar
1 garlic clove, peeled and split
½ teaspoon salt
3 cups cold cooked rice, long-grain Carolina or
    Italian imported (see cooking instructions page 181)
6 to 8 scallions, finely minced
8 to 10 pimiento-stuffed olives, coarsely chopped
½ cup Vinaigrette Dressing (recipe page 123)
3 pounds boiled jumbo shrimps, peeled and deveined
Lettuce
Mayonnaise Rouge (recipe follows)

Place the corn in a small saucepan and add water to cover. Bring to boil and cook uncovered for 3 minutes. Drain the corn and return it to the saucepan. Add the vinegar, garlic, and salt. Let stand at room temperature for about 1 hour (or cook ahead and refrigerate overnight). Drain; remove and discard garlic.

Combine corn with rice, minced scallions, and chopped olives. Add the vinaigrette dressing and gently toss and mix with 2 forks. Transfer mixture to a large shallow lettuce-lined bowl.

Arrange shrimps on rice. Spoon *mayonnaise rouge* over shrimps just before bringing to the buffet table.

MAKES ABOUT 12 SERVINGS.

MAYONNAISE ROUGE

Combine ¾ cup mayonnaise, ¼ cup chili sauce, and 1 teaspoon lemon juice; blend well.

MAKES 1 CUP.

◆

BASQUE SALAD

1 can (1 pound) green beans, drained
1 jar (1 pound) baby carrots, drained
8 to 10 boiled new potatoes, peeled and sliced
1 cup Parsley French Dressing (recipe page 68)
1 can (1 pound) sliced beets
Bibb lettuce, sufficient to cover a long oval platter
2 hard-cooked eggs, cut into quarters
1 flat tin (2 ounces) anchovy fillets
1 flat tin (about 4 ounces) Portuguese sardines
2 tomatoes, cut into wedges
2 tablespoons capers
Black olives

Combine beans, carrots, and potatoes in a bowl. Add ¾ cup of the French dressing. Pour remaining dressing over beets in a separate bowl. Cover bowls and refrigerate for several hours.

Make a bed of shredded lettuce on a long oval platter. Drain vegetables and place in separate rows across lettuce-lined platter. Arrange egg quarters around edge of platter. Top each with an anchovy fillet. Place sardines and tomato wedges between rows of vegetables. Sprinkle salad with capers and garnish with black olives.

MAKES 8 TO 12 SERVINGS.

◆

CUCUMBER MOUSSE WITH
MARINATED TOMATOES

3 packages (3 ounces each) lime-flavored gelatin
1 envelope unflavored gelatin
3 chicken bouillon cubes
2 cups boiling water
1 cup cold water
6 tablespoons tarragon vinegar
3 cups sour cream
½ cup diced radishes
1 cup diced cucumber
½ cup diced green pepper
Marinated Sliced Tomatoes (recipe follows)
Carrot curls

Dissolve lime-flavored gelatin, unflavored gelatin, and bouillon cubes in boiling water. Add cold water and vinegar. Blend in sour cream. Chill until thickened. Add remaining ingredients except tomatoes and carrots. Pour into 2 prepared 1½-quart molds. Chill until firm.

Unmold onto 1 long lettuce-lined platter or onto 2 round platters. Surround with marinated sliced tomatoes with parsley and chives. Garnish with carrot curls.

MAKES 8 TO 10 SERVINGS.

NOTE: Extra unflavored gelatin keeps this salad firm for several hours after unmolding.

MARINATED SLICED TOMATOES

3 *large ripe but firm tomatoes*
1 *garlic clove, peeled and cut into halves*
1 *small red chili pepper, minced and seeded (optional)*
¼ *cup mild salad oil*
2 *tablespoons apple-cider vinegar*
1 *tablespoon sugar*
1 *teaspoon salt*
¼ *teaspoon coarse-ground black pepper*
1 *small bunch of parsley*
8 *or 10 chives*
Lettuce

Drop the tomatoes into a large pan of boiling water for about 15 seconds. Plunge immediately into cold water, then slip off the skins. Cut each into halves and gently squeeze out the seeds. Cut each half into 2 or 3 slices. Place slices in a long shallow glass pan. Add garlic and chili pepper. Combine oil, vinegar, sugar, salt, and pepper. Beat with a whisk or fork until blended. Pour over tomato slices. Cover the pan with foil and refrigerate until about 1 hour before serving. Let stand at room temperature until ready to serve.

Mince the parsley and chives very fine. Remove tomato slices from marinade with a fork. Let drain briefly over pan. Arrange slightly overlapping on lettuce-lined salad platter. Sprinkle generously with parsley and chives.

MAKES 4 SERVINGS IF SERVED AS A SEPARATE DISH, BUT WILL GARNISH LARGER AMOUNTS.

◆

AVOCADO SALAD WITH
AVGOLEMONO SAUCE

3 large ripe but firm avocados
Lemon juice
3 hard-cooked eggs
Lettuce leaves
2 egg yolks
1 tablespoon Dijon-style mustard
1 teaspoon salt
¼ cup lemon juice
½ cup heavy cream
1 small jar (4 ounces) pimiento strips
1 tablespoon minced chives

Cut each avocado into halves, remove seeds, and peel. Cut each half lengthwise into 4 pieces. Sprinkle with lemon juice to prevent discoloration. Quarter the hard-cooked eggs. Arrange avocado slices and quartered eggs alternately on a lettuce-lined platter.

Beat egg yolks only until blended. Add mustard and blend well. Season with salt. Add the lemon juice, then the cream, beating with a wire whisk after each addition. Pour mixture over both avocado slices and egg wedges. Place slices of pimiento over each and sprinkle with chives.

MAKES 6 SERVINGS.

◆

FRENCH EGG AND POTATO SALAD

2 pounds boiling potatoes
4 tablespoons white-wine vinegar
4 hard-cooked eggs
1 teaspoon Dijon-style mustard
6 tablespoons mild salad oil
¼ cup minced chives or finely minced green onion
Salt
Freshly ground black pepper
Mayonnaise, if desired
Lemon juice
Lettuce leaves
Tomato wedges
Thin slices of raw zucchini
Black olives

Boil the potatoes in water to cover until done but not oversoft. Peel while still hot and cut into large dice. Sprinkle with 2 tablespoons of the vinegar. Toss gently with 2 forks. Set aside at room temperature.

Remove the yolks from the hard-cooked eggs and mash with the mustard and remaining vinegar. Mix in the oil to make a smooth dressing. Add this to the potatoes. Chop the hard-cooked egg whites and add. Add the minced chives. Again blend gently, using 2 forks, until potato cubes are coated with dressing and chives are evenly distributed. Add salt and pepper to taste. Cover and refrigerate for several hours, or until ready to serve.

If a more moist salad is desired, add a little commercially prepared mayonnaise mixed with a little fresh lemon juice.

To serve, bring salad to almost room temperature and correct seasoning with additional salt if needed. Mound potato salad in the center of a large lettuce-lined platter. Arrange alternate mounds of tomato wedges and zucchini slices around potato salad. Garnish with black olives.

MAKES ABOUT 8 SERVINGS.

◆

RUSSIAN SALAD PLATTER

2 *cups dried white beans*
1 *large onion, peeled and quartered*
¼ *teaspoon salt*
1 *cup each of the following vegetables:*
    Green peas
    Diced carrots
    Chopped green beans
Mayonnaise
Salt
Halves of hard-cooked eggs
Sour cream
Minced chives
Black and green olives

DRESSING
½ *cup mild salad oil*
1 *teaspoon sugar*
1 *teaspoon salt*
½ *teaspoon pepper*
¼ *cup tarragon vinegar*
2 *to 3 tablespoons minced chives*

Soak beans in water to cover overnight. Drain and place in a large pot. Cover with fresh water; add the quartered onion and salt. Cook over moderate heat until tender, about 45 minutes. Drain and place in a large bowl. Cook the peas, carrots, and beans separately until barely tender.

Combine dressing ingredients and blend well. Pour over beans and vegetables. Toss gently. Cover and refrigerate for several hours.

When ready to serve, drain off all excess dressing and add mayonnaise to taste. Correct seasoning with additional salt if needed. Arrange on a lettuce-lined platter. Surround with halves of hard-cooked eggs covered with sour cream and chives. Garnish platter with jumbo black and green olives.

MAKES 8 TO 12 SERVINGS.

◆

FOUR-BEAN SALAD
WITH VODKA AND SOUR CREAM

1 can (1 pound) red kidney beans
1 can (1 pound) cut green beans
1 can (1 pound) lima beans
1 can (1 pound) cut wax beans
½ cup chopped celery
½ cup chopped green pepper
Russian Dressing (recipe follows)
¼ cup vodka
Lettuce
¼ cup sour cream
½ cup sliced pitted ripe olives
½ cup sliced pimiento-stuffed green olives

Drain beans and combine in a large mixing bowl with the celery and green pepper. Add Russian dressing. Using 2 forks, mix gently but thoroughly. Refrigerate for several hours to blend flavors and chill.

To serve, add vodka to salad and again toss and blend gently but thoroughly. Transfer to a lettuce-lined platter. Spoon sour cream over surface. Sprinkle ripe and green olive slices over sour cream.

RUSSIAN DRESSING

1 teaspoon dry mustard
1 teaspoon white-wine vinegar
2 teaspoons grated horseradish
1 tablespoon minced green onion
1 tablespoon minced parsley
1 teaspoon salt
¼ cup chili sauce
1½ cups mayonnaise
1 teaspoon lemon juice

Mix the mustard with the vinegar. Stir in the horseradish, green onion, parsley, and salt. Blend well. Add the chili sauce, then the mayonnaise and lemon juice. Blend thoroughly.

MAKES 1½ CUPS.

◆

PART III:
DESSERTS FOR A COCKTAIL BUFFET

◆

PEACH TRIFLE

6 to 8 large ripe peaches
Lemon juice
4 eggs
1 cup sugar
1 envelope unflavored gelatin
¼ cup cold water
¼ cup Grand Marnier liqueur
1 cup whipping cream
12 to 14 petit beurre or tea biscuits or vanilla wafers

Peel and slice peaches; sprinkle with lemon juice. Refrigerate covered until ready to use. Beat eggs in top of double boiler until blended. Add sugar and beat over, not in, simmering water until mixture has tripled in volume and has become a light and fluffy custard that does not separate. Dissolve gelatin in cold water and add to hot custard, blending well. Remove from heat and add liqueur. Cover and cool to room temperature.

Whip cream until stiff. Fold into the cooled custard. Crumble *petit beurre* or tea biscuits or vanilla wafers and use to cover the bottom of 6 to 8 individual custard bowls or 1 large one. Cover with the sliced peaches. Pour in custard. Cover and refrigerate until time to serve.

MAKES 6 TO 8 SERVINGS.

◆

MOCHA MOUSSE

4 eggs
1 cup sugar
3 ounces (3 squares) unsweetened chocolate
1 envelope unflavored gelatin
⅓ cup cold coffee
1 cup sour cream
¼ cup light rum
8 to 10 thin chocolate wafers
Whipped cream

Break eggs into the top part of a double boiler. Beat with a whisk until blended. Add sugar. Place over, not in, simmering water. Beat with a whisk until mixture has about tripled in volume and has become a fluffy and light custard. Meanwhile, place chocolate on a sheet of lightly buttered foil. Bring up edges of foil to form a shallow bowl. Place in a pan in a 350° F. oven until chocolate has melted. Scrape melted chocolate from foil into custard and beat until blended.

Sprinkle gelatin over cold coffee in a small saucepan and stir over low heat until dissolved. Add to custard and beat until blended. Fold in sour cream and rum.

Cover the bottom of a 2-quart soufflé mold with chocolate wafers, filling in the spaces between whole wafers with broken wafers. Line sides of mold with a ring of wafers. Gently pour in custard. Refrigerate until firm and well chilled. Garnish with whipped cream just before serving.

MAKES 6 TO 8 SERVINGS.

◆

CHEESE PIE GRAND MARNIER

1½ cups graham-cracker crumbs
2 tablespoons confectioners' sugar
⅓ cup melted butter, cooled
3 eggs
9 ounces cream cheese, at room temperature
½ cup granulated sugar
3 tablespoons Grand Marnier liqueur
1 cup commercial sour cream
2 tablespoons brown sugar

Preheat oven to 350° F.

Combine 1 cup crumbs with the confectioners' sugar and melted butter. Mix thoroughly. Spread and press mixture on buttered sides and bottom of a 9-inch pie pan. Refrigerate until chilled.

Beat eggs slightly, add cream cheese, and blend well. Add granulated sugar gradually, beating after each addition. Blend in Grand Marnier. Pour mixture into crumb-lined pan. Bake in preheated oven for 20 minutes, or until firm. Cool.

Mix together sour cream and brown sugar and spread over surface of pie. Place in freezer until topping is firm. Wrap pie in foil, seal, and store in freezer.

Remove from freezer and let stand at room temperature for about 30 minutes before serving.

MAKES 6 TO 8 SERVINGS.

◆

COINTREAU PIE

½ *pound shelled Brazil nuts*
¾ *cup sugar*
2 envelopes unflavored gelatin
½ *cup cold water*
1½ *cups milk*
3 eggs, separated
⅛ *teaspoon salt*
½ *cup chopped candied orange peel*
¼ *cup Cointreau liqueur*
1 cup heavy cream

Preheat oven to 400° F.

Grind nuts in food grinder or use electric blender. Measure; you should have about 1¾ cups nuts. Combine 1½ cups ground nuts with ¼ cup of the sugar. Press onto bottom and sides of a 9-inch pie pan up to the rim with the back of a wooden spoon. Bake in preheated oven for 10 minutes. Set aside.

Sprinkle gelatin over cold water in a large bowl. Heat milk to boiling point. Beat egg yolks with ¼ cup of sugar and the salt. Slowly add hot milk, beating as it is added. Pour into pan in which milk was heated. Cook, stirring almost constantly, over low heat until mixture thickens and coats the spoon. Pour over softened gelatin, stirring as it is added. Cool slightly. Add orange peel and Cointreau. Cover surface with plastic wrap and refrigerate until thick (a small amount will mound when dropped from a spoon). Beat with a wire whisk for about 1 minute.

Beat egg whites until stiff. Add remaining ¼ cup sugar, 1

tablespoon at a time. Fold into custard mixture. Pour into cooled pie shell. Chill. Pie can be made 1 day ahead to this point.

Whip cream and spread on pie. Sprinkle with remaining Brazil nuts. Refrigerate until time to serve.

MAKES 6 TO 8 SERVINGS.

◆

COMPOTE OF EXOTIC FRUITS

2 large fresh pineapples
1 can (4 ounces) white pitted lichees in syrup
1 bottle (4 ounces) kumquats in syrup
1 jar (4 ounces) Mandarin orange sections
1 large bunch of white seedless grapes
½ cup Kirsch

Peel the pineapples and cut into slices; trim brown spots from edge of each slice and cut each into 4 wedges. Cut out and discard hard core from each wedge. Drain canned and bottled fruits. Reserve juices. Place all fruits in an attractive serving bowl and mix gently.

Combine juices and add enough of the mixture to the bowl to moisten fruit. Add Kirsch. Cover bowl and refrigerate until well chilled, or until ready to serve.

MAKES 8 TO 12 SERVINGS.

Dinner
Parties

As a professional person your time is your capital, and you must plan your investment of it carefully. After all, there are just so many after-working hours to spend each week and so much that you really want to do with them. Does this mean that because you have a career you can't have the fun of cooking and serving great party meals? Not at all. Between *haute cuisine* and "just heat and eat" there are any number of satisfactory ways to prepare really memorable food.

First, dismiss the idea that all great cuisines are based on slowly cooked foods. It's simply not true, as anyone who knows the preparation time for most fine Chinese dishes will enthusiastically testify.

Second, forget the old-fashioned American blue-plate notion that every dinner party menu must begin with cocktails, then soup or appetizer, go on to meat, potatoes, vegetables, salad, and bread, and end with an elaborate dessert.

Instead, begin by expanding your knowledge of quality foods. With shopping expertise the best costs little more than second rate, and it's not only how you cook but the ingredients you buy that make for superior dining.

Next, learn about the great classic convenience foods that have been used for hundreds of years by knowledgeable French and continental cooks and professional chefs: fine cheeses, fresh fruits, and honest breads. Add to this a knowledge of the best of both imported and domestic packaged, frozen, and canned foods.

Then, finally, learn to combine these good things creatively with your own *spécialités de la maison*, the excellent dishes you cook expertly at home. The results can be spectacular.

For instance, your Italian-inspired supper party can begin with a really great antipasto—an assortment of Italian-style sausages and breads, plump black olives, sardines in mustard, rolled anchovies, white-meat tuna in olive oil, pimientos, peppers, and more—all purchased from an Italian grocery or the gourmet department of a really good supermarket. With it serve carafes of garnet-red Chianti. Your guests circle the laden table, choose, fill their glasses, talk, and blissfully munch; then they return for seconds while you cook, very quickly because you are expert and all ingredients are ready and waiting, a simply superb *fettucini Alfredo*. Bring it to the table steamy hot and fragrant, with freshly grated Parmesan cheese, each strand of pasta rich with sweet butter and cream. Everyone loves it. Because you have cooked something very special, especially for them, it's a party, festive and fun.

The meal ends with a mellow dessert cheese and fresh fruits, espresso coffee, Italian cookies, relaxed talk, and more talk.

The end result—a very special evening, and it happened not because you spent a lot of money or slaved all day over a hot stove, but because you knew what to buy, how to cook one effective dish, and how to present the meal effectively. Such results can be achieved for any type of party meal. It's a formula that can be adapted to any life-style, any house or apartment, and any budget—large, medium, or small.

◆

INDIAN CURRY DINNER

THE MENU

*Broccoli Vinaigrette
with Capers and Tomatoes*

*Bombay Chicken Curry
Rice*

Accompaniments

Chutney	*Chopped Parsley*
Chopped Scallions	*Chopped Hard-Cooked Eggs*
Flaked Coconut	*Chopped Peanuts*

Cold Beer

*Adele's Frozen Rajah Pudding
Coffee*

Cognac

Everything can be made ahead for this menu. The chicken and stock for curry can be made up to a week ahead; if your guests are asked on short notice, both bottled or canned chicken and canned chicken broth can be substituted. The accompaniments, except for the hard-cooked eggs, scallions, and parsley, come already prepared; the frozen dessert might be one you made weeks before for just such an occasion.

ABOUT BROCCOLI VINAIGRETTE

This is an especially good choice for an easy first course that takes the place of a salad. Actually, it must be made ahead for full flavor so make it the night before, cover tightly, and refrigerate until just before serving. Frozen broccoli can be substituted, but thaw for about 30 minutes before cooking, and cook only until barely tender. This is a good-looking salad that needs no garnish; just drain well and arrange on plates.

ABOUT CHICKEN CURRY

The curry can be made as much as a week or two ahead and frozen, well wrapped, until ready to reheat and serve. Reheat slowly in a saucepan set in a larger pan of simmering water. Transfer to a heated serving dish to bring to the table.

If time is of the essence, you can use cans or jars of best-quality chicken and chicken stock, or prepare your own chicken and stock a week or more ahead.

ABOUT CURRY POWDER

The top secret to a great curry dish is the curry powder used. Curry powder is not one spice, but a blend of spices. There are several excellent brands on the market. All contain a large percentage of turmeric, which gives the characteristic goldenrod yellow hue, but apart from that each powder is different from others in flavor, color, and intensity. Some of the spices included are cardamom, coriander, mustard and allspice.

If the brand you buy proves too mild for your taste, you can step up the flavor by adding your own spices—a touch of saffron if you can afford it, a bit of chili, and a pinch of ginger will give character to less-inspired and inexpensive blends.

ABOUT RICE

Converted precooked rice presents no problem and is literally foolproof if package directions are followed precisely, but it's fun to explore other varieties of rice occasionally. I often use the short stubby grains from Piedmont in Northern Italy. It has such superb flavor that I am frequently asked for the recipe. Long-grain Carolina rice is also delicious and has an interesting texture. The thin-grain rice from India is also good, but there are many others. As all rice can be prepared ahead and kept hot or reheated, none of them presents a real problem in cooking. Though each variety absorbs a different amount of water and the cooking time varies considerably, you can't fail if you follow the same basic rules in cooking: use at least 4 cups of water for each cup of rice. Add 1 teaspoon of salt and 1 tablespoonful of oil. Bring the water to a full boil before adding the rice and let bubble gently. Test frequently as the rice cooks and stop the cooking precisely when the rice is done, which means when each grain is tender but still firm.

Drain the rice into a colander which has been placed in the sink. If you turn on the cold tap water you will prevent steam from rising into your face.

To keep drained rice warm, rinse out the pot, fill with about 2 inches of water, and place over low heat. Put the colander of rice over, not in, the water and cover it with a damp paper towel. Remoisten the paper if it dries out completely.

To reheat, pour boiling water over the rice in the colander, then drain and replace the colander over low heat. Rice will be hot in 5 to 10 minutes. There's a bonus in this steaming: it assures that the rice will be dry and fluffy with no trace of stickiness.

Rice will stay hot over steam, without becoming too dry, for about 1 hour.

ABOUT CURRY ACCOMPANIMENTS

Scallions are scallions and need only to be trimmed, washed, patted dry, and chopped. The same goes for the parsley. The best peanuts are the dry-roast kind, unsalted of course. They should be coarsely chopped.

The coconut problem is solved by buying a box of shredded coconut; just make sure you get the unsweetened variety. Bottled chutney can be purchased almost anywhere. This leaves you with only the task of boiling, cooking, peeling, and chopping the eggs.

One final note: all accompaniments can be prepared ahead and placed in separate covered containers. The best place to store them is in the refrigerator, obviously, but do remember to bring them to room temperature before they are served or they will cool down the curry and rice as soon as they are added to the serving plates. For this menu I serve the accompaniments from separate small bowls, but they could also be effectively arranged in separate rows across a long platter.

ABOUT BEER

Like ham with eggs, red wine with crusty bread and cheese, beer teams up with curry. Though many Indians are content to sip tea and some wine buffs will tell you that chilled Chablis is the logical choice, to my mind beer is the only beverage that is sufficiently robust to stand up to the intense flavor of any curry dish. My choice is a light pale ale. Serve it well chilled, of course, but not overchilled. If you have purchased your supply some days ahead, store it in a cool, dark place, then place it in the refrigerator 4 or 5 hours before serving. Too cold beer will not foam well; if insufficiently chilled, it will foam too much.

To serve, hold bottle close to rim of glass and pour beer slowly down the inside against the glass until about three-quarters full, then pour quickly into the center of the glass to obtain a cap of foam. You can pour the beer yourself just before you bring the hot food to the table, but curry is a thirsty dish and most people will want more than 1 glass, so it's a good idea to have several open bottles handy, kept cold in an ice-filled wine bucket, though any large deep bowl will suit the purpose just as effectively.

ABOUT DESSERT AND COFFEE

The dessert for this menu is an easy but spectacular finale. Make ahead and freeze in individual soufflé molds; just remember to take it from the freezer about 30 minutes before serving.

The coffee can also be made ahead and kept hot. Warm the cognac, so as not to chill the coffee, in a pan of hot water. Bring the cognac to the table in its own bottle along with the coffee, or pour the coffee into large demitasse cups and add a teaspoon of warm cognac to each.

◆

BROCCOLI VINAIGRETTE
WITH CAPERS AND TOMATOES

1 *bunch (about 1½ pounds) broccoli*
2 *small onions, peeled and cut into very thin slices*
2 *tomatoes, peeled, seeded, and diced*
2 *tablespoons capers*
½ *cup salad oil*
¼ *cup vinegar*
2 *teaspoons sugar*
½ *teaspoon salt*
½ *teaspoon black pepper*
½ *teaspoon dry mustard*

Cut off tough stems and wash the broccoli well in a large bowl of salted water; rinse thoroughly and drain. Separate into serving-sized stalks. Place in a large sauté pan with a tight-fitting lid and add sufficient water to cover the bottom of the pan by about ½ inch. Cover tightly and cook over high heat until water starts to steam; cook for 1 minute longer and remove from heat. Let stand covered for a moment or two longer, then drain and place in a shallow nonmetal dish; a glass baking dish is ideal.

Break onion slices into rings and add, along with tomatoes and capers, to broccoli. Combine remaining ingredients in a small bowl and blend well. Pour over vegetables; toss to distribute dressing. Cover and refrigerate for at least 3 to 4 hours. Drain before serving.

MAKES 6 SERVINGS.

◆

BOMBAY CHICKEN CURRY

4 tablespoons butter
1 tart apple, peeled, cored, and finely diced
2 small white onions, peeled and minced
¼ teaspoon salt
¼ teaspoon black pepper
1 tablespoon curry powder
2 tablespoons flour
3 cups clear chicken broth, fresh or canned
3 cups bite-sized pieces of cooked chicken, fresh or canned
2 tablespoons sour cream

Melt butter in a heavy saucepan, add diced apple and minced onions, and cook over very low heat until soft but not brown. Stir in salt, pepper, curry powder, and flour. Continue to cook for 1 or 2 minutes longer. Add chicken broth, a little at a time, blending until smooth. Bring mixture to a full boil, then reduce heat to just barely simmering. Cook for 30 to 40 minutes, or until sauce has thickened to a creamy consistency. Add chicken and cook for an additional 10 to 15 minutes, or until chicken is very hot. Stir in sour cream. Serve over freshly cooked white rice with accompaniments (suggestions follow).

MAKES 6 SERVINGS.

ACCOMPANIMENTS

2 cups chopped unsalted dry-roasted peanuts
1 cup finely chopped parsley
1 cup minced green onion
3 hard-cooked eggs, finely chopped
1 cup shredded unsweetened coconut
1 cup Major Grey chutney

You'll need a 4½- to 5-pound chicken to obtain the 3 cups diced chicken (no bones or skin) needed for this curry dish, but this same chicken will give you at least twice the needed stock for future use.

◆

POACHED CHICKEN AND STOCK
A DAY-OFF-FROM-WORK RECIPE

4- to 4½-pound chicken, cut into 8 pieces
3 quarts water, more if needed
2 garlic cloves, peeled
1 carrot, scraped
1 celery rib with leaves
1 onion, peeled and quartered
A few mushroom and parsley stems (optional)
½ to 1 cup dry white wine or dry vermouth

Put chicken pieces into the water in a large pot, bring to a boil, and skim surface until clear. Add all remaining ingredients except wine. Reduce the heat so that the liquid barely simmers. Cook until chicken is tender enough to remove easily from the bone, about 1 hour.

Remove chicken pieces from stock and let stand until cool enough to handle. Remove skin and bones. Cut into generous bite-sized pieces. Place in a bowl and add about ½ cup of the stock, enough to moisten. Cover the bowl and refrigerate until ready to use.

Return all of the bones and skin to the stock and add the wine. Let simmer gently for about 2 hours.

Let the stock cool slightly, then strain it through a fine sieve into a large bowl. Refrigerate until all of the fat has come to the surface and congealed. This will take several hours. I usually prepare stock 1 day ahead, then remove the fat next morning. The stock will have jellied and can be stored as is in the refrigerator for several days before using, or it can be reheated into liquid, poured in 1- or 2-cup widemouthed containers, sealed, and stored in the freezer for 4 to 6 weeks.

◆

ADELE'S FROZEN RAJAH PUDDING

12 ounces sour cream
2 tablespoons brown sugar
1 pint orange sherbet
1 package (10 ounces) frozen raspberries,
*   partially thawed*
6 tablespoons macaroon crumbs (optional)

Combine sour cream with brown sugar; blend well. Place a layer of sherbet about 1½ inches thick in the bottom of 6 individual soufflé dishes; cover with a layer of raspberries, then fill to rim with sweetened sour cream. Sprinkle with macaroon crumbs if desired and freeze until firm. If dessert is to be made ahead, cover puddings securely once they have frozen firm.

MAKES 6 SERVINGS.

◆

NEAR EASTERN COOKOUT

Dolmadakia
Greek Salad
Barbecued Lamb Near East Style

Light Red Wine

Pilaf with Chick Peas
Armenian Flat Bread
Baklava

Greek Coffee

This menu is festive and fun with very little work involved. The *dolmadakia* come in jars and need only to be drained and arranged on a plate. Flat bread labeled "Armenian" or "bread of the Middle East" is available in the freezer department of most supermarkets; it needs only to be heated. The *phyllo* pastry leaves or their acceptable substitute, strudel dough, will also be in the same general section.

The *baklava* can be made a day or two ahead and stored in the refrigerator. The lamb can be marinated until ready to roast; salad ingredients can be prepared and stored in the refrigerator. The pilaf and chick peas can be made several hours before serving. That leaves only the salad to assemble at the last minute.

ABOUT DOLMADAKIA

Dolmadakia are grape leaves stuffed with a spicy lamb and rice mixture. They can be made at home, but the process is time-consuming, and unless you use the bottled-in-brine grape leaves you don't have the real thing. As the bottled stuffed leaves cost no more than the plain ones, I buy my *dolmadakia* already prepared. Expensive? Rather, but 1 small jar is all you need to make 6 to 8 servings as an appetizer, and they do add an authentic touch to a Greek party. You'll find them in gourmet food shops as well as in Greek groceries.

ABOUT LAMB

When buying, look for lean, light pink, smooth-textured meat. The older the lamb the darker the meat and the less delicate the flavor. Genuine spring lamb is from 3 to 5 months old; just plain lamb is a few months older. Over 20 months, it's mutton.

However you cook lamb—for this party it's cooked on an outdoor grill—don't overcook! It tastes best well browned on the outside, faintly pink in the center.

◆

GREEK SALAD

Sufficient mixed greens, Boston or Bibb lettuce, escarole,
    romaine, etc., torn into bite-sized pieces to make
    about 4 cups torn greens
4 small cucumbers, peeled
8 to 10 scallions, finely minced
2 large ripe tomatoes
1 large purple onion
1 flat tin (2 ounces) anchovies
1 jar (8 ounces) Greek black olives
½ pound feta cheese
Olive oil and anchovy oil to make about ⅓ cup
2 tablespoons lemon juice
Salt
Pepper
Oregano

Wash all greens, blot dry, and tear into bite-sized pieces. To store, wrap loosely in cold wet paper toweling and place in refrigerator.

Trim and peel cucumbers; cut into thin rounds. Mince

scallions fine. Peel tomatoes and cut each into 6 or 8 wedges. Peel onion, cut into thin slices, and break slices into rings. Drain anchovies, reserving oil. Drain olives. Crumble cheese.

Just before serving, place all greens in a large salad bowl. Combine olive oil and reserve anchovy oil. Add to greens and toss until each leaf is coated with oil. Add lemon juice and sprinkle lightly with salt, pepper, and a pinch of oregano. Add remaining ingredients. Toss again and serve.

MAKES 6 SERVINGS.

◆

BARBECUED LAMB NEAR EAST STYLE

1 leg of lamb, about 6 pounds
1 cup olive oil
⅓ cup fresh lemon juice
1 teaspoon salt
1 teaspoon Madras curry powder
½ teaspoon coarse-ground black pepper
3 garlic cloves, peeled and split
2 tablespoons butter
2 tablespoons coarse salt

Have the butcher bone the leg of lamb and shape it so that the meat lies flat in one long piece (butterflied). It will be raggedy and uneven, unattractive to say the least, but don't let that worry you. It will look fine when cooked and, what's more important, it will taste superb.

Place the meat, boned side up, on a cutting board; with a sharp knife remove any clumps of fat. Turn it over. If the butcher has not done so, peel off the fell (the parchmentlike covering) and remove all but a thin layer of fat. Place the meat in a long shallow nonmetal pan. Combine remaining ingredients except butter and coarse salt, and pour over surface of meat. Marinate the lamb for 12 to 24 hours, turning occasionally. Place it in the refrigerator if you like, but remove it and let stand at room temperature for as long as possible, preferably 6 to 8 hours, before cooking.

Bring the butter to room temperature until it is very soft and spreadable. Take the meat from the marinade and drain but do not dry it completely; slash edges in several places.

Arrange the meat, fat side up, on an adjustable outdoor grill about 4 inches above glowing hot coals. Watch it carefully (coals are unpredictable). After about 15 minutes the underside should be nicely browned and lightly charred in places. Using tongs—not a fork, which would pierce the meat and result in a loss of juices—turn the meat and grill for a final 10 to 12 minutes. The surface of the lamb should be crusty brown, the center pink and juicy.

Spread the soft butter over a long serving platter and sprinkle with the salt.

Place the meat on a cutting board and allow to stand for about 10 minutes, then carve it against the grain, as you would a London broil, in ¼-inch-thick slices. Arrange the slices, slightly overlapping, over the buttered and salted platter, and pour whatever juices have collected on the cutting board over the surface. Serve as soon as possible.

As a boned leg of lamb prepared in this way is uneven, thick in some places, thin in others, slices will be a mixture of rare, medium, and well-done, so that guests can select their preference.

MAKES 6 OR MORE SERVINGS.

◆

PILAF WITH CHICK PEAS

PILAF
2 cups clear chicken stock or broth
2 cups water
4 tablespoons butter
½ cup finely chopped onion
2 cups uncooked long-grain converted rice or Italian rice
Salt
Pepper

Combine stock and water in a saucepan and heat to boiling. Keep hot. Melt butter in a second heavy saucepan, preferably ceramic-coated cast iron. Add the onion and stir over moderate heat until limp. Add the rice and continue to stir until each grain is coated with butter. Pour in the hot stock and water. Let simmer over low heat until almost all liquid has been absorbed and rice is tender. Cover the pan and place in a preheated 300° F. oven. Bake, covered, for 10 minutes, or until all liquid has been absorbed, or set aside until time to reheat.

CHICK PEAS
 2 garlic cloves, peeled and split
 2 tablespoons minced onion
 4 tablespoons olive oil
 1 can (1 pound, 4 ounces) chick peas
 2 tablespoons lemon juice
 Salt
 Pepper
 ½ cup chopped minced parsley

Cook the garlic and onion in the olive oil over low heat until onion is limp. Add chick peas and about ½ cup of liquid from the can. Let simmer until almost all liquid has been absorbed, about 15 minutes. Remove and discard garlic. Add lemon juice and season with salt and pepper. Stir in parsley and serve over or with pilaf. Chick peas can be prepared ahead and reheated.

MAKES 6 SERVINGS.

◆

BAKLAVA

 ½ pound butter
 ½ pound phyllo pastry sheets
 1 cup finely chopped walnuts
 ¾ cup sugar

Melt the butter in a small saucepan. With a pastry brush coat the bottom and sides of a long shallow baking pan with melted butter. Arrange 10 sheets of the pastry in the bottom of the pan, brushing each second sheet lightly with butter. Sprinkle with about ⅓ of the walnuts and ⅓ of the sugar. Repeat twice, ending with pastry.

With a sharp knife cut *baklava* into diamond-shaped pieces. Heat any remaining butter until it begins to brown and pour over surface of each piece.

Bake in a preheated 350° F. oven for 30 minutes. Reduce heat to 275° F. and continue to bake for 45 minutes longer. Cool slightly.

SYRUP

2 *cups sugar*
2 *cups water*
2 *tablespoons lemon juice*
2 *cloves*
1 *teaspoon grated lemon rind*

Combine ingredients in a saucepan and cook, stirring, over moderate heat until sugar has dissolved. Let simmer for 15 minutes. Remove and discard cloves. Pour very hot over *baklava*.

MAKES 8 SERVINGS.

NOTE: Frozen packaged strudel dough can be substituted for *phyllo* pastry leaves.

◆

GREEK COFFEE

2 *teaspoons ground Greek or Turkish coffee*
½ *teaspoon sugar, or to taste*
½ *cup water*
1 *thin twist of lemon peel*

Make the coffee in either a Greek or Turkish coffee pot, or in a small saucepan with a pouring lip. Serve in demitasse cups.

Put the coffee and sugar in the pot or saucepan and add the water. Place over medium heat and stir for a few seconds, then let come to a full boil. The mixture will boil up (and over unless you watch it). When it reaches the rim of the pot remove it immediately and pour the frothy mixture into the cup. This is the "cream." Return the pot to the heat and allow to boil to the rim once again.

Allow to settle, then pour over the "cream" to the rim of the cup. Drop a twist of lemon peel into the cup. Allow to stand for a few moments. Greek coffee is never stirred but sipped carefully without disturbing the grounds that have settled to the bottom of the cup.

MAKES 1 SERVING.

◆

DINNER PARTY
IN THE ITALIAN MANNER

THE MENU

Antipasto

Pasta with Sauce
Grated Parmesan Cheese
Garlic Bread

Zuppa Inglese
Tangerines and Peanuts

Chianti

Espresso Coffee

Anisette

Amarettes
(crisp Italian cookies)

These are such easy meals to prepare that it hardly seems possible that they could be so good. Typically Italian, they are friendly menus ideally suited to casual entertaining. In each case, the antipasto can be placed on the table along with the cheese, bread, and wine. As the sauce and pasta take only minutes to prepare, you can enjoy this first course with your guests, then cook the main course while they sip a second glass of wine.

ABOUT QUICK-COOKING PASTA DISHES

These are not original recipes but versions of Italian classics. They take only minutes to prepare but must be served as soon as cooked and must be served very hot.

Before your guests arrive have all ingredients prepared and assembled near the stove. Fill the pot for cooking the pasta with water and place it over low heat. This way you can bring it to a boil quickly. Bring a tablespoon of butter to room temperature and place it in the serving dish. Put both serving dish and entree plates in a 200° F. warming oven.

After guests have eaten the first course or are enjoying a second serving, cook the sauce or reheat the previously cooked sauce, then keep it hot while you boil the pasta. Have a colander ready in the sink to drain pasta as soon as it is done, just tender with no taste of flour. Shake the colander so that no trace of water remains to dilute the sauce. Transfer drained pasta to the hot buttered serving dish. With 2 forks lift and toss to distribute butter evenly. Add sauce and again toss and lift to distribute sauce. Serve at once, with a big bowl of freshly grated Parmesan cheese, crusty bread, and red wine.

ABOUT COOKING PASTA

Use a pot that is large enough to allow the pasta to swirl around in the water as it cooks. Use at least 2 quarts of water for each 8 ounces of pasta. Bring the water to a full rolling boil; add 1 teaspoon salt and 1 teaspoon of oil or butter.

Add long round pasta, such as spaghetti, a small bunch at a time, lowering it gently into the water as it softens. Add noodles only by the handful. The point is to keep the water boiling as the pasta is added.

Cooking time varies considerably depending on type of pasta. All pasta is at its best *al dente,* which loosely translated means slightly firm to the bite.

Start testing a few minutes before time listed on package directions for "done," as this tends to be overlong. Test by tasting —it's the only way. When the flour taste is no longer evident and the pasta is resilient but not oversoft, remove the pot from the heat and immediately dump the contents into a colander waiting in the sink. (If you let cold water run to the side of the sink, not into the colander, you will prevent any steam rising into your face.)

Shake pasta dry; don't rinse it! Then transfer it to a large warm buttered platter or bowl. Pour hot sauce over the pasta and quickly turn and lift until nicely mixed. Work quickly so that everything stays hot, and serve at once.

Pass grated Parmesan cheese and let each person add his own to taste.

If the pasta is cooked before you are ready to serve it, don't add the sauce; just dot it with slivers of room-temperature butter, which will keep it from sticking together. Cover the bowl or platter with foil, seal it airtight, and place in a 200° F. oven. It will keep "servable" for 20 to 30 minutes.

Reheat the sauce to boiling hot just before adding to the pasta.

ABOUT PARMESAN CHEESE

True Parmesan cheese is Italian. Though there are several packaged, bottled, grated domestic cheeses on the market labeled "Parmesan," they are not the same thing. Italian Parmesan, encased in a smoky black rind, is pale gold in color and delicately grained. Its flavor is unique, unmistakable. It's earthy yet piquant and vaguely sweet.

The best way to obtain really good Parmesan is to select your own imported Italian cheese at a reliable cheese shop or the gourmet cheese department of a top-quality supermarket. Ask to taste before you buy.

◆

PASTA CON RAGU ALLA BOLOGNESE

2 tablespoons butter
¼ pound prosciutto or Canadian bacon, finely minced
¼ pound fresh mushrooms, finely chopped
1 medium-sized onion, peeled and minced
1 jar (1 pound) Italian-style tomato sauce with meat
½ cup heavy cream, at room temperature
1 to 1½ pounds thin spaghetti, just cooked
      and still hot
Salt
Freshly ground black pepper
Parmesan cheese

Melt the butter in a saucepan. Add the minced prosciutto or bacon, the chopped mushrooms, and minced onion. Sauté for 8 to 10 minutes, or until onion is very limp. Add sauce and stir until blended. Stir in cream. Heat until steamy hot. Don't allow to boil after adding cream.

Pour over just-cooked very hot spaghetti. Sprinkle with salt and pepper. Serve at once with grated Parmesan cheese and pass additional cheese at the table.

MAKES 6 SERVINGS.

◆

SPAGHETTI WITH TOMATO SAUCE
AND ITALIAN SAUSAGE

1 tablespoon olive oil
1 small onion, peeled and chopped
1 garlic clove, peeled and cut into halves
2 medium-sized fresh tomatoes, chopped
1 can (1 pound) Italian-style tomato sauce
1 teaspoon tomato paste
2 or 3 dashes of Tabasco
Salt
*¾ to 1 pound Italian sweet or hot sausage, cooked and
    sliced*
1½ pounds thick spaghetti, just cooked and still hot

Heat the oil in a large saucepan over medium heat and add the
onion and garlic. Cook, stirring, until onion is limp. Add the
chopped tomatoes and tomato sauce, and stir in the tomato paste.
Season with Tabasco and salt to taste. Let simmer, stirring often,
for about 10 minutes. Add the sausage slices and cook for another
5 minutes. Keep hot or reheat. Pour very hot over just-cooked
spaghetti and serve at once.

MAKES 6 SERVINGS.

◆

GREEN NOODLES WITH BUTTER-CREAM
SAUCE AND BLACK OLIVES
AN ADAPTATION OF FETTUCCINE ALFREDO

1 small can (3¼ ounces) pitted black olives
¼ pound butter
½ cup grated Parmesan cheese
¼ cup heavy cream
1½ pounds flat green noodles, just cooked and still hot
Salt
Freshly ground black pepper

Drain the olives and coarsely chop them. Bring butter to room temperature. Cream until smooth, then add cheese, a little at a time, alternately with the cream, beating well after each addition. Fold in chopped olives.

Sprinkle hot noodles liberally with salt and pepper. Then add butter-cream sauce. Lift and turn noodles quickly to distribute sauce. Serve at once, with additional Parmesan cheese to sprinkle over each serving.

MAKES 6 SERVINGS.

♦

NOODLES WITH PRIMAVERA SAUCE

2 *pounds ripe tomatoes*
1 *small bunch parsley*
8 *to 10 scallions*
1 *small jar (6 to 8 ounces) pitted black olives*
6 *tablespoons butter*
1 *tablespoon crumbled fresh basil*
1 *teaspoon dried oregano*
Salt
Coarsely ground black pepper
1½ *pounds noodles, just cooked and still hot*
¼ *pound shredded mozzarella cheese*
Grated Parmesan cheese

Using a long-handled fork, plunge each tomato into a pan of boiling water for about 20 seconds. Hold under cold water and slip off skins. Cut into halves and gently squeeze out seeds. Cut into thin strips and drain in colander. Wash parsley, blot dry, discard tough stems, and chop fine. Wash, blot dry, trim, and coarse-chop scallions. Drain and coarse-chop olives.

Melt butter over moderate heat in a heavy frying pan. Add scallions and cook, stirring, for 2 or 3 minutes. Add tomatoes, olives, and herbs. Stir and cook until tomatoes are well heated, about 3 minutes. Season with salt and pepper to taste. Keep hot or reheat briefly just before using.

At serving time stir in chopped parsley and shredded mozzarella cheese. Pour over just-cooked hot noodles, toss to blend, and serve at once, with plenty of grated Parmesan cheese to sprinkle over each serving.

MAKES 6 SERVINGS.

◆

ZUPPA INGLESE

1 8- or 9-inch sponge cake, made from a mix or bought
　from a bakery
¾ cup light rum
⅓ cup sugar
4 egg yolks
¼ cup flour
½ teaspoon grated lemon rind
2 cups milk
¼ teaspoon vanilla
1 tablespoon butter
½ pint heavy cream
2 tablespoons confectioners' sugar
Maraschino cherries
Candied citron

Cut the sponge cake into 2 even layers. Place one layer in the bottom of a deep 8- or 9-inch glass serving bowl (or use a soufflé dish). Sprinkle ¼ cup rum over the surface. Set aside. Reserve second cake layer.

Combine sugar, egg yolks, flour, and lemon rind in a saucepan. In a separate pan heat the milk to almost boiling. Slowly add the hot milk to the sugar mixture, stirring as it is added. Cook, stirring, over low heat until thick and smooth. Remove from heat; add the vanilla and butter. Stir until butter is melted. Pour half of this custard into the serving bowl over cake layer. Top with reserved cake layer. Sprinkle cake with ¼ cup rum. Pour remaining custard over second cake layer. Refrigerate until cold.

Whip cream until stiff. Fold in remaining rum and confectioners' sugar. Spread over top of chilled cake. Decorate with maraschino cherries and candied citron. Refrigerate until time to serve.

MAKES 6 TO 8 SERVINGS.

◆

SEATED DINNER PARTY SPANISH-STYLE

THE MENU

Dry Sherry

Almonds
Pimiento-Stuffed Green Olives

Jellied Gazpacho Salad
Arroz con Pollo Estilo Peruano
or
Picadillo

Spanish Red Wine

Thick Slices of Crusty Bread

Guava Shells with
Brandied Cream Cheese
Water Biscuits
or
Brandied Flan
Coffee

This is another cook-ahead meal with almost no last-minute preparation. The salad can even be unmolded onto serving plates before guests arrive, to be returned to the refrigerator until time to serve.

The main dish, either the *arroz con pollo* or *picadillo*, can be brought to room temperature after being stored in the refrigerator or freezer; all that's required is reheating.

I prefer the guava shells, cream cheese, and crackers to the flan after these fairly substantial main courses; it need only be arranged for serving. If you like a sweeter ending, the flan is also a made-ahead dessert.

About sherry, see page 91.
About cooking rice, see page 181.

◆

JELLIED GAZPACHO SALAD

4 cups canned tomato juice
3 garlic cloves, peeled and chopped
1 celery rib, chopped
1 small white onion, peeled and chopped
1 bay leaf
3 envelopes unflavored gelatin
½ cup cold water
½ cup fresh lemon juice
1 tablespoon Worcestershire sauce
4 to 6 dashes of Tabasco
Salt
1 cucumber, peeled and finely chopped
1 tart apple, peeled, cored, and finely chopped
4 celery ribs, finely chopped
Lettuce

Combine tomato juice, garlic, 1 celery rib, the onion, and bay leaf in a saucepan. Let steam over low heat, without boiling, for about 15 minutes. Strain. Reheat liquid almost to boiling point.

Sprinkle gelatin over cold water in a large mixing bowl and let stand until softened, about 3 minutes. Add the strained hot tomato juice, and stir until gelatin has dissolved. Add lemon juice, Worcestershire sauce, and Tabasco. Taste and add salt as needed. Pour into a second cold bowl and refrigerate until mixture thickens. Add chopped cucumber, apple, and celery. Pour into 8 individual molds that have been lightly oiled with vegetable oil. Chill until firm, 2 hours or longer.

Unmold onto lettuce-lined salad plates.

MAKES 8 SERVINGS.

◆

ARROZ CON POLLO ESTILO PERUANO

3 to 4 pounds chicken legs and thighs, cut into
    serving pieces
Flour
Salt
Pepper
Cooking oil
3 tablespoons butter
½ cup chopped onion
½ cup chopped mushroom caps
1 garlic clove, peeled and minced
½ teaspoon ground saffron
1 tablespoon flour
2 large tomatoes, peeled, seeded, and chopped
2 cups chicken stock
½ cup dry white wine
½ pound chorizos (Spanish sausage), sliced, or
    substitute hot Italian sausage
1 pound jumbo shrimps, peeled and deveined
1 pint large oysters, drained
Cooked dry white rice (see cooking instructions page 181)

Dredge chicken pieces with flour mixed with salt and pepper. Heat the oil in a large heavy skillet until almost smoking. In it brown the chicken pieces, a few at a time. Remove as browned to a hot platter and set aside.

When all are browned pour off and discard cooking oil and add butter to the skillet. Melt over low heat, then add onion, mushrooms, and garlic. Stir in the saffron and flour; when blended, add tomatoes, stock, and wine. Bring to a boil, stirring, then add the chorizo slices and the browned chicken. Cover the skillet and let cook over low heat until chicken is tender, about 45 minutes. Can be made ahead to this point.

Add shrimps and oysters. Stir them down into the sauce and let simmer until shrimps are pink. Correct seasoning with additional salt if needed. Serve over hot fluffy dry rice.

MAKES 8 SERVINGS.

◆

PICADILLO

2 *tablespoons corn or safflower oil*
4 *tablespoons butter*
1 *small green pepper, seeded and minced*
1 *large purple onion, peeled and chopped*
1 *garlic clove, peeled and minced*
2 *pounds top round of beef, ground*
2 *cups diced cooked ham*
1 *can (19 ounces) tomatoes*
1 *can (17 ounces) kidney beans, drained*
1 *teaspoon salt*
1 *tablespoon chili powder*
1 *large avocado*
2 *firm bananas*
2 *tablespoons lemon juice*
Hot cooked rice (see cooking instructions page 181)

Heat oil with 1 tablespoon butter in a large skillet over medium heat. When the butter has melted, add the green pepper, onion, garlic, and beef. Cook, stirring, until meat is lightly browned. Add ham, tomatoes, beans, salt, and chili powder. Let simmer for about 45 minutes, stirring occasionally. If mixture becomes too thick, add about ¼ cup water.

Peel and seed avocado and cut lengthwise into ½-inch slices. Peel bananas and cut into halves, then cut lengthwise into 2 pieces. Melt remaining 3 tablespoons butter in a large skillet. Add avocado and banana slices in a single layer. Sprinkle with lemon juice. Cover and cook only until heated.

Arrange hot cooked rice on a long platter. Spoon *picadillo* over rice. Place avocado slices down the center of the *picadillo* and surround with banana slices.

MAKES 8 SERVINGS.

◆

GUAVA SHELLS AND
BRANDIED CREAM CHEESE

1 can (1 pound) guava shells
8 ounces cream cheese
2 tablespoons heavy cream, more if needed
2 tablespoons brandy

Chill the guava shells. Bring cream cheese to room temperature. Add the heavy cream and blend. Add the brandy and beat with a fork until light and fluffy, adding more cream if needed. Place a small mound of mixture on each dessert plate.

When ready to serve, surround with 2 or 3 guava shells and spoon about 1 tablespoon of syrup over each. Serve with water biscuits or other unsalted crackers. Provide each guest with both a small dessert knife and a dessert fork.

MAKES 8 SERVINGS.

◆

BRANDIED FLAN

5 eggs
1½ cups light cream
½ cup cognac or other good brandy
1½ cups sugar

Beat the eggs in a large bowl until blended. Add cream, cognac, and ½ cup sugar. Beat with a whisk until sugar has dissolved. Place a 10-inch-square baking pan on the middle rack of the oven. Pour in water to a depth of 1 inch.

Preheat oven to 350° F.

Put remaining sugar in an 8-inch-square Corning casserole or other dish that can be used both on top of the stove and in the oven. Place over medium heat and stir with a wooden spoon until sugar melts and becomes a pale golden syrup. Remove from heat; using 2 kitchen towels or potholders, rotate pan so that syrup coats bottom and sides evenly. Set aside until syrup hardens and cools slightly.

Pour egg mixture into syrup-lined pan. Set it gently in the pan of water in heated oven. Bake until firm, or until a knife inserted in center will come out clean, about 30 minutes.

MAKES 8 SERVINGS.

◆

DINNER PARTY
IN THE ORIENTAL MANNER

Egg Rolls
Sesame Shrimps
Barbecued Miniature Spareribs
Stir-Fried Pork and Vegetables
Rice

Cold Pale Ale
or
Well-Chilled White Wine

Soy Sauce
Plum Sauce
Mustard Dip

Preserved Kumquats
Fortune Cookies
Almond Cookies

I like to serve this meal "Chinese restaurant-style"—the table completely set and a small bowl of rice just to the right of each plate; next to the rice even smaller bowls holding individual portions of soy sauce, plum sauce, and mustard dip. All of the main-course dishes are on the table in Canton-style covered serving dishes.

There is some last-minute cooking involved here, but it's quick and easy if you follow this general timetable. Use frozen egg rolls. For the sesame shrimps, use the recipe on page 148.

COOKING SCHEDULE

One Day Ahead

Cook the rice (see cooking instructions page 181). Store in covered dish in refrigerator.

Wrap barbecued spareribs in foil and store in refrigerator.

Advance Preparation on the Day

Early in the day: Clean shrimps, place in marinade in shallow nonmetal baking dish, cover with foil, refrigerate.

Prepare—cut or chop—all vegetables and meat for stir-fry dish.

Place kumquats in individual serving bowls, spoon a little syrup over each, cover bowls with foil, refrigerate.

Refrigerate wine or ale.

Set the table.

About 1 hour before guests arrive: Take all food except kumquats from refrigerator to come to room temperature.

About 30 minutes before guests arrive: Dump rice into a colander and place over a pot of simmering water. Cover with damp paper toweling.

Pour dipping sauces into individual bowls and place on table.

Place cookies in a napkin-lined basket.

Arrange ingredients for stir-fry dish in order of use on a table near the stove.

Start reheating spareribs.

After Guests Arrive and about 20 Minutes
Before Serving the Meal

Start baking frozen egg rolls.

Broil shrimps. Place in serving dish. Keep warm on electric hot tray.

Cook stir-fry dish.

Take egg rolls from oven.

Sequence of the Meal

Transfer hot cooked stir-fry dish, spareribs, and egg rolls to serving dishes. Bring with shrimp dish to the table.

Spoon hot rice into individual bowls and bring to table.

Open wine or ale. Bring to table and fill glasses. Place second opened bottle of wine or bottles of ale on sideboard in ice bucket.

Dinner is ready.

◆

CHINESE-STYLE BARBECUED MINIATURE SPARERIBS

3 racks of small spareribs
1 teaspoon five-spice powder (optional)
½ cup good-quality barbecue sauce
¼ cup hoisin sauce
4 garlic cloves, peeled and minced
½ cup Mirin (Japanese rice wine) or dry sherry
1 teaspoon ground ginger

Have your butcher cut each rack of spareribs into 2 pieces across the bone, giving you 6 racks of miniature ribs. Arrange on a rack in a baking dish. Sprinkle with five-spice powder or MSG. Bake at 300° F. for 30 minutes.

Combine remaining ingredients and spread ribs with mixture. Bake for 30 minutes, brushing with sauce several times during baking. Ribs can be kept warm in a 200° F. oven or can be reheated in a 300° F. oven for about 15 minutes.

MAKES 6 SERVINGS.

◆

CHINESE-STYLE STIR-FRIED PORK
AND VEGETABLES

1 package (6 ounces) frozen snow peas
3 celery ribs
3 medium-sized white onions
1 large carrot
1 medium-sized white turnip
2 or 3 pieces of preserved-in-syrup ginger, well drained
10 to 12 canned water chestnuts
½ pound fresh young spinach
2 tablespoons corn or safflower oil
¼ cup chicken stock or broth
1½ to 2 cups diced roast pork
¼ cup soy sauce
Steamy hot white rice, freshly prepared or
*   reheated leftovers*
Crisp packaged Chinese noodles
Soy sauce

Remove snow peas from package and let stand at room temperature until ready to use. Wash celery and cut diagonally (at a 45-degree angle) into thin slices. Peel the onions, cut into quarters, and pull each quarter apart into "leaves." Scrape the carrot and cut it diagonally (at a 45-degree angle) into oval slices as thin as possible. Peel the turnip, cut into thin slices, and cut each slice into thin matchstick slivers. Slice the ginger and water chestnuts into thin slivers. Wash spinach, blot dry, remove and discard tough stems.

Heat the oil in a large, deep, heavy skillet over medium heat. Add the celery, onions, carrot, and turnip. Stir to coat vegetables with oil. Cover and let steam briefly. Add stock and stir to blend. Cover and let steam for 4 or 5 minutes. Add ginger, water chestnuts, and pork. Again stir to blend. Cover and cook for 4 or 5 minutes. Vegetables should be tender but with still a trace of crispness. Add snow peas, spinach, and ¼ cup soy sauce. Blend, cover, and steam for a final minute, or until spinach just begins to wilt.

Serve with steamy hot boiled rice. Sprinkle Chinese noodles over each serving and pass additional soy sauce at the table.

MAKES 4 SERVINGS.

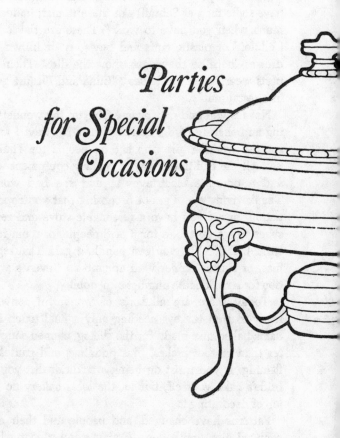

Parties
for Special
Occasions

We've all known those dreary office souls who wouldn't dream of having a traditional Christmas or Thanksgiving dinner at home. As for giving a wedding reception, they would think you were out of your mind. "No," they sigh, "Herbert and I will just have something at Schrafft's or the Automat; holidays don't mean much when you have to work." These are the ladies who wear Celluloid or plastic cuffs and buy gray or brown synthetic knit dresses "because they don't show the dirt." Their male counterparts wear green eyeshades ("Edna and I'll just grab something in a restaurant").

Not for you and not for me. Give up the wonderful, warm giving and sharing of the holiday feast? No way! I know one high-spirited working girl who had 12 people for Thanksgiving dinner. All she had in the way of cooking equipment was a hot plate and a portable electric oven, and she had worked overtime Thanksgiving eve. I'm not proposing that you cope with this situation, but if you have a reasonable stove and refrigerator and space to set up tables for 6 or 8 people, or room for a generous-sized buffet table, you can handle a gala Thanksgiving, Christmas, or Easter dinner with aplomb . . . even a wedding reception for a reasonable number of people.

Today there are all sorts of wonderful convenience foods, ready-roasted turkeys needing only a final touch for perfection, hams baked and ready for the slicing, canned soups that are better than mother makes, plus puddings and fruitcakes ready for flaming. If you insist on being a traditionalist you can bake the bride's cake yourself, but let the local bakery do a professional job of decorating it.

Patterns have changed, and people and their appetites have changed along with them. Today many a young bride wants to be married in a gingham dress, wearing a straw hat wreathed in fresh daisies. Why not a picnic wedding reception? In a country field with long tables set with picnic fare, a wonderful country pâté, a great cheese, the wedding cake, an applesauce cake, spicy and fragrant with raisins and walnuts. It's today's life-style.

Even the traditionalists are happy with elegant fare scaled to seventies proportions. Gone are the days when a full-scale dinner or elaborate luncheon was the only thing any self-respecting bride could accept. The formal wedding reception suggested here fulfills all the requirements for a gala feast. Delicious and delicate, it is still easy to handle even if time, space, and money are limited.

The point is not to give up the pleasure and satisfaction of holidays at your house simply because you work for a living. The ultimate joy of preparing your own daughter's wedding feast, the sense of participating in your own traditions that you alone create for yourself, your family, and your friends, is well worth the effort involved. No restaurant meal or "catered affair" can take their place.

To Grandma's (the fashion stylist's) New York apartment we'll
go for:

◆

AN OLD-FASHIONED CHRISTMAS DINNER
(PREPARED WITHOUT OLD-FASHIONED HOURS IN THE KITCHEN)

THE MENU

Champagne

Ripe Olives   Almonds
Jellied madrilène à la Russe
Thin-Sliced Black Bread
Spread with Sweet Butter

Roast Madeira-Glazed Turkey
Eggplant and Oyster Casserole
Green Beans Amandine
with Tomato Slices
Cranberry-Horseradish Mold

Champagne

Whiskey-Flamed Plum Pudding
with Whiskey Sauce
Coffee

ABOUT MADEIRA-GLAZED TURKEY

Buy a bird rotisserie-roasted, but slightly undercooked, at the
best delicatessen in town. Reheat on a rack in a roasting pan in
a 350° F. oven for 45 minutes to 1 hour, basting frequently with
Madeira wine. Prepare 1 hour ahead and leave at room temperature until time to bring to the table and carve, which will leave
the oven free for baking the vegetables.

ABOUT GREEN BEANS AMANDINE WITH TOMATOES

Use "frozen" green beans amandine, 1 package for each 2 servings. Top each package with 2 thick slices of ripe tomato, sprinkled with salt and sugar, and dot generously with butter. Bake until beans are bubbly hot and tomato slices soft.

ABOUT PLUM PUDDING

Buy very good pudding from a specialty shop or the delicacy department of a good department store. Heat it and flame with bourbon whiskey. The sauce is made with the same potent brew.

◆

JELLIED MADRILÈNE À LA RUSSE

2 Belgium endives
3 cans (13 ounces each) jellied madrilène, *well chilled*
Juice from 1 large lemon
1 cup sour cream
1 small can (4 ounces) caviar

Cut off tough ends of endives and separate leaves. Wash under cold water. Pat dry with paper toweling. Trim off bottom of each leaf. Line 8 individual soup cups with endive tips so that tips extend evenly about ½ inch above rims of cups. Fill lined cups with chilled *madrilène*. Squeeze a little lemon juice over each serving. Top each with 2 tablespoons sour cream and sprinkle with the caviar, evenly divided among the cups.

MAKES 8 SERVINGS.

♦

EGGPLANT AND OYSTER CASSEROLE

1 large eggplant
½ cup water
1 small white onion, peeled and chopped
¼ pound butter
1½ cups crumbled corn bread, homemade or
    made from a mix
½ teaspoon salt
¼ teaspoon pepper
2 eggs, well beaten
1 pint oysters
Paprika

Prepare this on the day ahead, bake, cool, and refrigerate. Reheat just before serving. Serve instead of turkey dressing.

Peel eggplant and cut into small cubes. Place in saucepan with the water. Cover and cook over low heat until eggplant is very soft. Check occasionally, and add 1 to 2 tablespoons more water if needed to keep vegetable from sticking. Remove from heat. Transfer to mixing bowl and mash to a pulp.

Sauté onion in butter until limp. Add to eggplant. Add remaining ingredients except paprika. Transfer to a well-buttered 2-quart casserole. Bake at 375° F. until firm, about 30 minutes.

After reheating sprinkle with paprika and serve from casserole.
MAKES 8 SERVINGS.

◆

CRANBERRY-HORSERADISH MOLD

1 package (3 ounces) raspberry-flavored gelatin
1 envelope unflavored gelatin
⅛ teaspoon salt
⅓ cup sugar
1 cup boiling water
2 cups cold water
1 medium-sized crisp apple
1 cup cranberries, fresh or frozen
2 tablespoons bottled prepared horseradish

Make this on the day ahead.

Combine flavored gelatin, unflavored gelatin, salt, and sugar in the container of an electric blender. Pour in boiling water and blend at low speed until gelatins have dissolved. Pour into a mixing bowl and add cold water. Measure out ½ cup and reserve. Chill remaining mixture until thickened.

Peel and core apple and cut into wedges. Combine apple wedges, cranberries, and reserved gelatin mixture in container of electric blender and blend at low speed until fruit is broken into pieces. Add horseradish. Stir into thickened gelatin. Pour mixture into a 1-quart mold and chill until firm. Unmold just before serving.

MAKES 8 SERVINGS.

◆

WHISKEY SAUCE
FOR
PLUM PUDDING

1 cup sugar
2 eggs, lightly beaten
4 tablespoons butter, melted and cooled
Bourbon whiskey

Combine sugar and eggs in top part of a double boiler over simmering water. Beat with a wire whisk until about triple in volume. Slowly add butter, beating as it is added. Let cool, then add bourbon to taste.

MAKES 3 CUPS SAUCE, OR MORE.

◆

SMALL COUNTRY WEDDING RECEPTION
(FOR 18 TO 24)

THE MENU

Country Pâté
Crusty French Bread   *Cornichon Pickles*

Ham Loaves Breton-Style

Red Wine

Wheel of Camembert Cheese
Unsalted Crackers
Baskets of Grapes

His and Hers Applesauce Cakes
Coffee

◆

COUNTRY PÂTÉ

2 pounds best-quality liverwurst, in 1 piece
½ pound butter
½ cup cognac or other good brandy
1 tablespoon Worcestershire sauce
2 tablespoons Dijon-style mustard
3 or 4 dashes of Tabasco
Salt
Paprika

Bring liverwurst and butter to room temperature. Place in a large mixing bowl and mash with a heavy spoon until blended and smooth. Add cognac, Worcestershire sauce, mustard, and Tabasco. Blend and add salt to taste. Pack in stoneware crocks or small earthenware bowls. Cover containers with foil and refrigerate pâté for 12 to 24 hours. Sprinkle with paprika just before serving.

MAKES 10 TO 12 SERVINGS. DOUBLE THE RECIPE FOR THE WEDDING RECEPTION.

◆

HAM LOAVES BRETON-STYLE

12 cups ground cured ham
12 cups ground lean pork
12 cups good-quality packaged seasoned stuffing mix
2 teaspoons pepper
14 eggs
2 quarts milk
1 cup firmly packed light brown sugar
¼ cup dry mustard
1 cup vinegar

Preheat oven to 375° F.

Oil well 4 loaf pans, each 9 x 5 x 4 inches. Combine ham, pork, and stuffing mix, and season with pepper. Beat eggs until blended, then combine with milk. Combine mixtures and blend thoroughly. Divide mixture equally among prepared pans. Combine sugar, mustard, and vinegar in a saucepan and stir over low heat until sugar has dissolved. Pour over ham loaves. Bake in preheated oven for 1 hour.

Cool to room temperature before slicing.

MAKES 24 SERVINGS.

◆

HIS AND HERS APPLESAUCE CAKES
A DAY-OFF-FROM-WORK RECIPE

3 *cups stone-ground whole-wheat pastry flour*
2 *tablespoons baking soda*
¼ *teaspoon salt*
2 *cups chopped walnuts*
2 *cups seedless raisins*
½ *cup butter*
¾ *cup light brown sugar*
2 *eggs*
2 *cups canned applesauce*
½ *cup cognac or other good brandy*

Preheat oven to 325° F.

Generously oil 2 loaf pans, each 9 x 5 x 3 inches. Dust with flour. Shake out excess flour. Dump flour, baking soda, and salt into a mixing bowl and mix thoroughly. Place nuts and raisins on a large sheet of waxed paper. Mix in about 1 cup of the flour mixture. In a separate bowl, cream butter with sugar until light. Beat in eggs. Beat with an electric beater or a wire whisk until sugar has dissolved. Fold in the flour mixture alternately with the applesauce. Fold in the nuts and raisins. Turn the batter into prepared pans and place in preheated oven. Bake for 1 to 1½ hours, or until cake is done—when a cake tester inserted in center comes out clean.

Cool slightly, then turn out onto a cake rack. With a small sharp knife make several deep slits in each cake. Sprinkle ¼ cup cognac over each cake. Cool completely. Wrap in foil and refrigerate or freeze until day of wedding.

Take to your bakery, the best in town, and have each cake iced and decorated in traditional wedding style.

MAKES 24 SLICES.

◆

FORMAL WEDDING RECEPTION
(FOR 20 TO 25)

THE MENU

Jellied Avocado Mousse
Homemade Melba Toast

Turkey and Fruit Salad with Curry Mayonnaise

Champagne Punch

Thin Bread-and-Butter Sandwiches
Traditional Wedding Cake

With a little planning you can prepare this menu in a leisurely way, at your own pace, starting several days ahead of the wedding.

Order the cake at least a week ahead from a bakery that will deliver it to your door; a decorated cake, even a small one, is difficult to transport so this job is best left to professionals.

Prepare the toast and sandwiches three days ahead. Store the toast at room temperature in an airtight container. Wrap the sandwiches in stacks in clean tea towels that you have rinsed in ice water, then firmly wrung out, until they are evenly moist but not the least bit "drippy." Place each stack in a plastic bag and store in the refrigerator.

Boil the turkey 2 days ahead, 1 day ahead prepare the salads and punch base.

There's really little else to do but set the table.

Open the Champagne, bring out the punch bowl, and you are ready for your guests.

◆

JELLIED AVOCADO MOUSSE

4 packages (3 ounces each) lime-flavored gelatin
2 envelopes unflavored gelatin
1½ teaspoons salt
4 cups boiling water
2¾ cups cold water
4 avocados
½ cup lemon juice
¾ cup mayonnaise

Dissolve gelatins and salt in boiling water. Add cold water. Chill until slightly thickened. Peel and seed avocados. Mash until smooth. Stir in lemon juice and mayonnaise, blending well. Fold into gelatin mixture. Pour into 2 6-cup ring molds. Chill until firm.

MAKES 18 TO 20 SERVINGS.

◆

TURKEY AND FRUIT SALAD
WITH CURRY MAYONNAISE

1 12- to 14-pound turkey
1 carrot, scraped
1 large onion, peeled and cut into quarters
3 garlic cloves, peeled
2 celery ribs with leaves
1 bay leaf
3 or 4 sprigs of parsley
1 tablespoon salt
6 large seedless oranges, peeled, and chopped
2 pounds seedless green grapes
1 small bunch of celery, thoroughly washed and chopped
8 ounces whole unblanched almonds
Curry Mayonnaise (recipe follows)
Salt
Crisp lettuce leaves

Have your butcher cut the turkey into pieces as he would a
chicken for frying.

Place turkey pieces in a deep soup kettle and cover with cold
water. Bring to a full boil and boil for about 5 minutes. Remove
turkey pieces, pour off water, and wash pot. Then return the turkey to the pot and add carrot, onion, garlic, celery ribs with
leaves, bay leaf, and parsley. Cover with water and add salt.
Bring to a boil, then reduce heat and let the turkey simmer until
the meat is tender enough to pull easily from bones, 2½ to 3
hours.

Remove from heat and allow to cool in the cooking liquid.
Remove all skin and bones. Place turkey meat in a nonmetal
bowl. Add sufficient cooking liquid barely to cover. Cover bowl
and refrigerate until ready to use.

Drain cooked turkey meat and pat dry. Cut into bite-sized

pieces. Place in a large mixing bowl. Add remaining ingredients except lettuce. Toss well. Add sufficient mayonnaise to moisten salad. Add salt to taste. Cover and refrigerate for several hours or overnight before serving.

Serve in a large lettuce-lined salad bowl.

MAKES 20 SERVINGS.

CURRY MAYONNAISE

To 1 cup mayonnaise add 1 teaspoon lemon juice and 1 tablespoon curry powder. Blend well. Double the recipe for 20 servings.

♦

CHAMPAGNE PUNCH

2 cups sugar
Juice from 6 large lemons
Juice from 6 large oranges
1 pint cognac
4 bottles domestic sweet sauterne
6 bottles Champagne, chilled

Dissolve sugar in lemon juice. Add orange juice, cognac, and sauterne. Chill thoroughly. When ready to serve, pour into punch bowl over block of ice. Pour in chilled Champagne.

MAKES 25 SERVINGS, 3 4-OUNCE SERVINGS PER PERSON.

◆

LARGE FAMILY REUNION PARTY
(FOR 35 TO 50)

THE MENU

Twelve-Boy Salad Table
Roquefort Dressing   Poppy-Seed Dressing
Creole French Dressing

Roast Shoulder of Beef
Cheese Tray
Assorted Crackers

Cokes   Beer   Red Wine

Baskets of Fresh Fruits

Assorted Cookies
Coffee

There's very little work involved in preparing this feast and a lot of fun. As for shopping, you'll find a good part of the menu packaged, prepared, ready to open and serve—in the gourmet department of your supermarket. Setting the table is no chore, and even the actual cooking is a breeze. The salad dressings are super easy to put together, and meat is roasted by a never-fail method that takes no effort on the part of the cook.

◆

TWELVE-BOY SALAD

Wash and pat dry sufficient mixed greens to fill 2 or 3 tremendous bowls, tossed with just enough salad oil to coat each leaf very lightly. Surrounded by bowls of any 12 of the following:

Garlic croutons
Rolled anchovy fillets
Julienne strips of Swiss cheese
Julienne strips of baked ham
Julienne strips of cooked chicken or turkey
Thin-sliced onion rings
Crisp crumbled bacon
Drained capers
Artichoke hearts
Sliced unpeeled radishes
Tomato wedges
Sliced raw mushrooms, sprinkled with lemon juice
Peeled and sliced avocado, sprinkled with lemon juice
Hard-cooked egg wedges
Ripe or green olives
Minced green pepper
Minced green onion
Minced parsley
Cold pickled beets
Asparagus spears
Cold green beans vinaigrette

Guests help themselves to greens, then add their own choice of accompaniments and dressing.

◆

ROQUEFORT DRESSING

2 cups mayonnaise
1 cup commercial sour cream
3 tablespoons freshly squeezed lemon juice
1½ cups crumbled Roquefort cheese
Salt
Pepper

Combine mayonnaise, sour cream, lemon juice, and cheese; mix well. Season with salt and pepper to taste. Refrigerate, covered, for several hours before serving.

MAKES ABOUT 3 CUPS.

◆

POPPY-SEED DRESSING

¾ cup sugar
1 teaspoon grated onion
½ cup tarragon vinegar
¼ cup fresh lemon juice
2 cups mild salad oil
1 teaspoon dry mustard
1 teaspoon paprika
¼ cup poppy seeds

Put all ingredients in a Mason jar. Cover and shake until well blended. Refrigerate for several hours before serving.

MAKES ABOUT 3 CUPS.

◆

CREOLE FRENCH DRESSING

2 cups salad oil
¾ cup vinegar
2 tablespoons sugar
1 tablespoon Dijon-style mustard
5 or 6 dashes of Tabasco
½ teaspoon Worcestershire sauce
1 garlic clove, peeled

Combine ingredients in a quart Mason jar and shake well. Refrigerate for several hours before serving. Remove and discard garlic after 2 or 3 hours.

MAKES ABOUT 3 CUPS.

◆

MARY HAGERTY'S
WHOLE SHOULDER ROUND OF BEEF

18 to 20 pounds whole round of choice beef
Freshly ground black pepper
Salt

Bring meat to room temperature; this requires several hours.

Preheat oven to 500° F.

Place meat on broiler rack and roast for 1 hour at 500° F. Reduce temperature to 200° F. and roast meat about 8 hours.

Remove from oven and sprinkle immediately with a generous amount of pepper and salt. Let meat stand at room temperature for at least 30 minutes before carving. Meat will stay warm, just right for eating, for several hours.

NOTE: You can put the meat in the preheated 500° F. oven about 9 o'clock in the morning. It will be ready for the table about 6 P.M. It will stay warm at room temperature 2 or 3 hours and can be served at room temperature.

EASTER DINNER

THE MENU

Jellied Easter-Egg Salad

Julio's Braised Shoulder of Lamb
Casserole of Potatoes in Cream
Steamed Broccoli

Dry Red Wine
French Bordeaux
or
California Cabernet Sauvignon

Red-Hot Pepper Jelly
Hot Rolls

Easter Bombe
Coffee

♦

JELLIED EASTER-EGG SALAD

AVOCADO EGGS

1 *cup mashed avocado* (1 *large or* 2 *small avocados*)

3 *ounces cream cheese, at room temperature*

½ *cup heavy cream*

¼ *cup mayonnaise*

½ *teaspoon salt*

2 *envelopes unflavored gelatin*

2 *tablespoons lemon juice combined with* 2 *tablespoons*
   cold water

Red caviar

Combine avocado, cream cheese, heavy cream, mayonnaise, and salt. Blend until smooth, by hand or in an electric blender. Sprinkle gelatin over lemon juice and water. Stir over simmering water until gelatin is completely dissolved. Stir into avocado mixture. Chill until mixture begins to thicken.

Pour about 1 tablespoon of the mixture into each "egg cup" of a 12-cup plastic egg tray. Sprinkle each with red caviar. Chill until firm. Fill each cup to brim with remaining avocado mixture. Chill until firm.

MADRILÈNE EGGS

½ envelope unflavored gelatin
2 tablespoons lemon juice mixed with 2 tablespoons
     cold water
1 can (13 ounces) jellied madrilène
Slivered black olives

Sprinkle gelatin over lemon juice and water. Stir over simmering water until gelatin is dissolved. Add to room-temperature madrilène. Chill until mixture begins to thicken.

Pour about 1 tablespoon of the mixture into each "egg cup" of a 12-cup plastic egg tray. Sprinkle with slivered black olives. Chill until firm. Cover with remaining madrilène mixture. Chill until firm.

TO PREPARE SALAD

Unmold eggs onto lettuce-lined individual salad plates. Garnish with mayonnaise.

MAKES 12 SERVINGS, OR MORE.

◆

JULIO'S BRAISED SHOULDER OF LAMB

¼ pound salt pork, cut into small dice
1 shoulder of lamb, 6½ to 7 pounds, boned and tied
3 tablespoons butter
2 garlic cloves, peeled and chopped
2 large purple onions, peeled and chopped
3 celery ribs, chopped
½ teaspoon coarse-ground black pepper
1 teaspoon salt
1 teaspoon mixed Italian herbs
1½ cups dry white wine
1 can (1 pound) stewed tomatoes with basil

Prepare ahead, then refrigerate or freeze until time to reheat.

Place pork dice in a small saucepan. Cover with water and bring to a boil. Let simmer for 5 minutes. Drain and pat thoroughly dry with paper toweling. Place in a large heavy flame-proof casserole over moderate heat until all fat has been rendered.

Remove and discard rendered pork dice from casserole. Heat rendered fat to almost smoking. Reduce heat to moderate. Add lamb and brown well on all sides. This will take about 15 minutes. Remove meat from casserole and set aside. Pour off and discard the fat.

Wipe out the casserole with paper toweling and add the butter, garlic, onions, and celery. Sauté over moderate heat until vegetables are limp.

Preheat oven to 375° F.

Place the browned lamb over the vegetables. Sprinkle with pepper, salt, and Italian herbs. Pour in the wine and tomatoes and bring liquids to a full boil. Cover meat loosely with foil. Cover casserole with a tight-fitting lid and place it in the preheated oven. Let meat cook for about 3 hours. Basting is not necessary.

Remove meat from casserole and let stand at room temperature for about 30 minutes. When cool enough to handle, wrap in foil and store in refrigerator until sauce is ready to use.

Strain sauce into a clean bowl, pressing down on vegetables to extract all liquid. Cool slightly, then refrigerate several hours, until all fat rises to the surface. Remove congealed fat from cold sauce.

Place meat on a carving board and slice carefully, using a long sharp knife. Lay meat slices slightly overlapping in a shallow au gratin or other baking dish. Pour strained sauce over surface. Can be made ahead to this point.

Reheat in 375° F. oven until sauce is bubbly hot, or cover dish with foil and refrigerate until ready to reheat.

MAKES 8 TO 10 SERVINGS.

◆

CASSEROLE OF POTATOES IN CREAM

2 cups light cream
1 cup beef or chicken stock or clear broth
4 tablespoons butter
Salt
Pepper
1 garlic clove, peeled and split
6 medium-sized baking potatoes
Buttered Bread Crumbs (recipe follows)

Combine cream, stock, and butter in a large saucepan. Season lightly with salt and pepper. Add garlic. Place over moderate heat. Peel potatoes and slice about ⅛ inch thick; drop each slice into the hot cream and stock as soon as sliced. Partially cover the pan and let cook over moderate heat until potatoes are almost but not quite soft. Test with the point of a small sharp knife. Remove and discard garlic.

Transfer potatoes and their liquid to a long shallow au gratin or other similar baking dish. Sprinkle evenly with buttered crumbs. Can be prepared ahead to this point. Cover baking dish with foil and store in refrigerator.

Bring to room temperature and set baking dish on a baking sheet. Place in a preheated 325° F. oven and bake until sauce has thickened and crumbs are lightly browned, about 30 minutes. Serve from the dish.

MAKES 8 TO 12 SERVINGS.

BUTTERED BREAD CRUMBS
2 tablespoons butter
1 cup (commercially prepared) fine dry bread crumbs

Melt butter in a small saucepan. Remove from heat and stir in bread crumbs.

Use as directed in recipe.

◆

STEAMED BROCCOLI

2 packages (10 ounces each) frozen broccoli
2 tablespoons butter
¼ cup water
1 teaspoon salt
2 tablespoons lemon juice
½ cup fine dry bread crumbs
Paprika

Let frozen broccoli thaw at room temperature for about 30 minutes. With a sharp knife cut flowerets from stalks. Cut stalks into slices about ½ inch thick.

Combine 1 tablespoon of the butter with the water and salt. Bring to a boil, then add sliced stalks. Cover and cook over medium heat for about 5 minutes. Add flowerets. Cover and cook for about 5 additional minutes, or until both stalks and flowerets are tender. Drain off any remaining liquid. Add remaining butter and lemon juice. Transfer to serving dish and sprinkle with bread crumbs and paprika.

MAKES 8 SERVINGS.

◆

RED-HOT PEPPER JELLY
A DAY-OFF-FROM-WORK RECIPE

2 cups unsweetened apple juice
1 cup apple-cider vinegar
5½ cups sugar
1 to 2 teaspoons Tabasco
1 bottle (6 ounces) liquid pectin
2 or 3 drops of red food coloring

Combine apple juice, vinegar, and sugar in a large saucepan and stir over medium heat until sugar has dissolved. Bring to a full boil, stirring constantly. Remove from heat. Add Tabasco and stir in pectin. Return to heat and bring again to a full rolling boil. Let boil for 1 minute. Remove from heat and stir in food coloring. Skim surface with a metal spoon. Pour into just-washed dry Mason jars. Seal.

MAKES ABOUT 4 PINTS.

◆

EASTER BOMBE

1 cup crumbled macaroons
½ cup orange liqueur (Grand Marnier, Cointreau, or other)
1 quart vanilla ice cream
1 quart orange sherbet
Candied violets (optional)

Combine crumbled macaroons and orange liqueur in a small bowl. Let stand for about 30 minutes.

Line a 2-quart oval mold with vanilla ice cream. Use a wooden spoon and your hands to pack down; work quickly. Fold macaroon crumbs into orange sherbet. Spoon into cavity of mold. Fill mold to top with vanilla ice cream, packing it down. Cover mold with foil and seal. Freeze until very firm.

To unmold, soak a clean towel in hot water, wring it out and wrap around the mold for about 15 seconds. Unmold onto serving platter. Sprinkle with candied violets if desired.

MAKES 10 TO 12 SERVINGS.

◆

FOURTH OF JULY PORCH PICNIC

THE MENU

Cheese Firecrackers
on Watercress with Unsalted Crackers

Cold Lemon-Baked Chicken

Coleslaw   *Macaroni Salad*   *Potato Salad*
Hot Homemade Rolls

Beer

Old-Fashioned Poundcake
Iced Tea   Coffee

◆

CHEESE FIRECRACKERS

8 ounces cream cheese
1 pound sharp Cheddar cheese, grated
2 tablespoons heavy cream
1 teaspoon Worcestershire sauce
2 or 3 dashes of Tabasco
2 tablespoons cognac
½ teaspoon salt
4 tablespoons paprika
3 tablespoons chili powder
4 thin carrot sticks, about 1 inch long
Watercress

Bring cream cheese to room temperature. Add Cheddar cheese
and cream. Blend with an electric mixer until smooth or cream
together with a heavy wooden spoon. Blend in Worcestershire,
Tabasco, and cognac. Season with salt. Mix paprika with chili
powder. Spread out on waxed paper. Dust hands lightly with
flour and shape cheese mixture into 4 logs, "firecracker" size,
about 1 inch in diameter. Roll in paprika and chili powder until
completely covered. Refrigerate, covered, until well chilled and
flavors have blended, 6 to 24 hours. Force a carrot stick "wick"
into one end of each log. Cover a platter with watercress and
arrange firecracker logs on top, in wheel spoke design. Serve
crackers separately.

EACH FIRECRACKER WILL MAKE ABOUT 4 SERVINGS.

◆

COLD LEMON-BAKED CHICKEN

3 broilers, 2 to 3 pounds each, each cut into 6 pieces
Salt
Lemon juice from 2 or 3 large lemons

Place chicken pieces skin side up in a single layer, not touching, in 1 or 2 long shallow baking dishes. Place in a preheated 350° F. oven and bake for 30 minutes. Turn each piece skin side down and sprinkle liberally first with salt and then with lemon juice. Bake for 15 minutes, then turn each piece again, and again sprinkle with salt and lemon juice. Bake for a final 15 minutes. Remove chicken pieces and drain on paper toweling. Cool to room temperature.

MAKES 6 TO 8 SERVINGS.

◆

ADELE'S COLESLAW

1 small head of cabbage
1 tart apple
1 firm pear
1 carrot
Juice from 1 lemon
Salt
Pepper
Mayonnaise

Cut cabbage into quarters. Wash and trim. Peel apple and pear; scrape carrot. Place cabbage, apple, pear, and carrot on a large chopping board and chop very fine. Place in a large bowl. Add lemon juice and season with salt and pepper. Add only enough mayonnaise to hold mixture together. Cover and refrigerate for several hours before serving.

MAKES 8 TO 10 GENEROUS SERVINGS.

◆

MACARONI SALAD

4 hard-cooked eggs
3 tablespoons vinegar
3 tablespoons prepared hot mustard
1 cup mayonnaise
½ teaspoon salt
1 pound uncooked elbow macaroni
1 cup finely sliced celery
½ cup finely chopped sweet mixed pickles
1 small jar (4 ounces) chopped pimientos, well drained
¼ cup minced green onions

Cut hard-cooked eggs into halves. Remove yolks. Reserve whites. Place yolks in a mixing bowl and mash. Blend in vinegar, mustard, and mayonnaise; season with salt.

Cook macaroni according to package directions. Drain and place in a large bowl. Add mayonnaise mixture and remaining ingredients. Toss to blend. Cover and refrigerate until about 1 hour before serving. Chop reserved egg whites and use as a garnish. This salad is best when served at room temperature.

MAKES 6 TO 8 SERVINGS.

◆

SOUTHERN POTATO SALAD

*6 to 8 large boiling potatoes, or sufficient to make 4 cups
   diced potatoes*
3 teaspoons salt
¼ cup white-wine vinegar
1 teaspoon dry mustard
¼ cup minced green onions
½ cup minced parsley
¼ cup chopped sweet mixed pickles
1 cup finely chopped celery
1 cup mayonnaise
1 tablespoon lemon juice

Peel potatoes and cut into generous bite-sized cubes. Bring a
large pot of water to almost boiling. Add the potatoes and 1 teaspoon salt; let boil until tender but not falling apart. Drain into
a colander, then return them to the pot and shake gently over
a low heat until each cube is dry.

Mix together the vinegar, 2 teaspoons salt, and dry mustard.
Pour over hot potato cubes. Stir and lift very gently until vinegar
has been absorbed. Refrigerate until well chilled.

Add remaining ingredients. Toss again to blend, taking care
not to mash or break up potatoes. Add additional salt if needed.
Cover and store in refrigerator if desired, but bring to room temperature before serving.

MAKES 8 TO 10 SERVINGS.

◆

OLD-FASHIONED POUNDCAKE
A DAY-OFF-FROM-WORK RECIPE

4 cups sifted all-purpose flour
1 teaspoon baking powder
Pinch of grated nutmeg
Pinch of salt
2 cups unsalted butter, at room temperature
3 cups sugar
6 large eggs
¾ cup light cream
¼ cup blended whiskey
½ teaspoon Angostura bitters
Powdered sugar

Butter and flour a 10-inch tube pan.

Preheat oven to 300° F.

Sift together the flour, baking powder, nutmeg, and salt. Cream the butter until very light and fluffy. Add the sugar, ¼ cup at a time, and beat well after each addition. Continue to beat until sugar has dissolved. (This is the real secret of a smooth moist cake.) Add the eggs, one at a time, beating well after each addition. Combine cream, whiskey, and bitters. Add the sifted flour mixture to the butter and egg mixture alternately with the cream mixture, beginning and ending with the dry ingredients. Spoon into the prepared pan.

Place in the preheated oven and bake for 1 hour and 20 minutes, or until cake just begins to shrink from the sides of the pan and a finger pressed gently in the cake leaves a print that vanishes slowly. Cool cake upright in its pan on a rack for 10 minutes, then turn out onto rack and cool to room temperature before slicing or wrapping and storing.

NOTE: Wrap securely in foil and store in refrigerator or freezer.
MAKES ABOUT 20 SLICES.

Index